THE STORY OF MUSIC

I.S. BACH.

Gemalt von Haußmann   gestochen von I. G. Bulow Leipz. 1774

THE STORY OF MUSIC

AN HISTORICAL SKETCH
OF THE CHANGES IN MUSICAL FORM

by PAUL BEKKER

Translation by M. D. HERTER NORTON and
ALICE KORTSCHAK

AMS PRESS
NEW YORK

Reprinted from the edition of 1927, New York
First AMS EDITION published 1970
Manufactured in the United States of America

International Standard Book Number: 0-404-00729-5

Library of Congress Card Catalog Number: 74-124592

AMS PRESS, INC.
NEW YORK, N.Y. 10003

PUBLISHERS' NOTE

The illustrations are reproduced from the collection of Mr. Joseph Muller of New York. The book is designed by Mr. Vincent Cicatelli. The Publishers gratefully acknowledge their obligation to both these gentlemen.

CONTENTS

ILLUSTRATIONS

FOREWORD

Two years ago, the Southwest German Radio Corporation asked me if I were prepared to give a series of lectures in the Radio High School on the history of music. There were to be some 20 lectures, each of a half hour's duration. At first I was doubtful whether to take up the suggestion. The lectures seemed to me too few and too brief for dealing with the subject, and moreover, as a self-taught individual, I felt some scruple about trusting myself in a matter which seemed to demand treatment by a professional historian of music. On the other hand, I had to admit that the present academic attitude toward music history is scarcely calculated to bring the subject nearer to the layman. It is quite possible—I say it without implying anything derogatory—that the painstaking philological studies carried on today by the musicologists are necessary and useful, and that after a time a constructive personality will appear among these learned gentlemen who will be able to correlate their work to some productive purpose. Meanwhile, since this individual is not at hand it remains for the unacademic person to choose whether he will modestly await his coming, or in all temerity set about making his own history of music.

I freely confess that I have chosen the second
course, not from any lack of modesty, but because I
believe that the presentation of history is a matter less
of knowledge than of *point of view*. For this reason
the invitation of the Radio Corporation attracted me
particularly, as it gave me the opportunity of testing
the soundness of the ideas developed in my book on
Wagner and my pamphlet on "The Nature of Tone"
in the larger field of music history as a whole. These
lectures, which were given under the title of "The
History of Change in Music," are here presented in
book form. While the title has been changed, the lec-
ture form has been retained because it gives the
original layout of the material.

I shall probably be accused of "construing" the
facts in my own way. I shall not dispute the accusa-
tion save to add that I know no presentation of history which is not a "construction" in this sense. Every
scientific theory is a construction—we should not
allow ourselves to be pleasantly misled as to the significance of alleged "facts." The question is not
whether facts are construed, but what is the *quality*
of the interpretation put upon them. If it leads to a
creative attitude, there must be something alive in it,
of which we must take heed, even though it may not
have received academic sanction.

I beg the musicologists to forgive me, to disdain me
if they must. No one is obliged to read my book;
whom it angers, let him lay it aside. Perhaps a few

readers may be found to whom it will give pleasure, and for these it is intended.

PAUL BEKKER.

Cassel, March 1926.

THE STORY OF MUSIC

CHAPTER I

HOW TO APPROACH THE HISTORY OF MUSIC

THE following pages were originally entitled "The History of Change in Music." The title was not chosen at random. It indicates the point of view from which I approach the material in hand, the process which we call music history, that is, the occurrence of events in music from its early beginnings as we know them to the present time. I do not intend to describe in detail the lives of individual composers or the great types of musical form as they appeared at different times and in different countries. An attempt to press so much into the limits of this volume would be doomed to failure, and even in other circumstances I would not venture upon such a task. For events and dates and the lives of famous musicians we may learn about in books. But there is something which as yet we cannot learn about in books, and that is, *how* to look at and understand music history as a whole.

When I say that Beethoven lived from 1770 to 1827, he was born at Bonn and died in Vienna, he wrote for the piano, voice and orchestra, he used mainly the sonata form; even when I explain these statements more exactly, I am only supplying knowledge which means little to the reader and which he will soon have forgotten. But if I try to explain just why at Beethoven's time piano chamber and orchestra music enjoyed such peculiar prominence, how the sonata form came to be so firmly established; if I endeavor to make intelligible the conditions governing historical occurrences; then, though the details of my exposition too will soon be forgotten, a different picture will remain. We shall see that history is not a collection of dates and incidents and so-called facts, but the great *life process* of mankind, which we may comprehend, not by looking at it as a kind of historical costume parade, but only by trying to recognize the forces which control it. The present book is written from this point of view, which, since it is not the customary way of regarding the march of events, I shall devote this first chapter to explaining.

When we open a history of music today we encounter the word *development* in every other sentence. Everything develops. Pre-Christian music develops into the polyphony of the Renaissance, vocal music develops into instrumental music, the symphony develops from the Mannheim school through Haydn and Mozart to Beethoven, the song develops from Schubert to Hugo Wolf, and so on. This is the usual manner of presentation, in which the simple always figures as the forerunner of the complex and the complex as an improvement over the primitive. This conception may be explained by recalling that the musical science of today is a product of the 19th century. The ideas of the 19th century were dominated by the theory of evolution. In the interpretation of this theory, however, there were undoubtedly misunderstandings. It is clear enough that a causal connection exists between the different stages of development, that each stage is an organic consequence of the preceding stage; and in making clear such relations, even between many great species which appeared fundamentally different, lay the extraordinary contribution of the theory of evolution. But the theory becomes unsound whenever it tries to make later developments appear necessarily *higher* in the sense of absolute improvement over what went before.

Here lies an error in interpretation. Since the constructive forces always remain the same, since nothing can be added or lost, it follows that the total value of the result must always remain the same too. Only *appearances* change, so that what takes place is a transformation and not a development. Goethe, who early grasped the idea of evolution, speaks not of the development of the plant but of its *metamorphosis*, the series of changes in the plant organism. This idea of metamorphosis as opposed to the idea of development we must accept as the basis of approach

to all history, especially the history of art. Men have
been men at all times, at least as clever, at least as
talented and as inventive as ourselves. We have no
right to look down on any former times and speak
of them as primitive. Though they had to do without
many things we consider essential to daily existence,
the people of those times in turn possessed qualities
which we do not appreciate only because, having
changed ourselves, we are no longer aware of them.
Development in the sense of progress, of higher
degree or improvement, I cannot admit; at least not
in works of art, in which I find only the metamorphosis of ceaselessly working forces. The concern of
history, therefore, lies not in presenting events themselves, but in making intelligible the laws and forces
which determine their *transformation*. In these laws
and forces life itself is at work, while events are
merely the effects of their activity.

So I shall discard the idea of development as misleading and put in its place that of metamorphosis,
of transformation. I beg the reader to keep in mind as
the basis for all further discussion of different periods
in history that the forms of art never develop, they
can only change; that the music of all times is artistically, absolutely, ever the same; that it always reflects
the nature of the people who created it; and that
we, finally, have no reason to believe that the intellectual and artistic capacities of the people of

former centuries were not at least as high as our own.

Another important point should be considered in the history of music; namely, that no other art has left us so inadequately informed about its past. This is primarily because of the nature of its material; for the material of music is tone and tone is vibrating air. The plastic arts work with stone, canvas and color; poetry works with thought which can be accurately written down. But how shall the works of an art which manifests itself in vibrations of air be preserved through thousands of years?

Music, of course, has also a written language in notation, but for exactness this does not compare with the written letter. Even today we are no longer in a position to say definitely how music was performed in the 18th century; nor can we be sure, in spite of all the notes in the world, what idea of tone Bach and Handel had in mind when they composed. And this difficulty is negligible compared with the difficulties we encounter as soon as we go back two or three centuries further, where the question of how the composer wanted his works performed, whether with voice alone or with instruments as well, gives rise to much learned dispute. This in turn appears trifling in comparison with times still more remote, where the simplest questions of rhythm, the duration of a single tone perhaps, can only be guessed at from the notation. And finally we come to a time where our nota-

tion does not yet exist, where note-writing consists of
so-called *neumes*, signs somewhat similar to our sten-
ography.

These neumes, which were in use until after the
11th century, differed in different times and places.
They have been deciphered with partial success, although this question also has aroused divergent opinions. All our knowledge is relative, at best, for the
only reliable test, the *practical* demonstration of ancient music, is no longer possible. We shall never
achieve an authentic idea of how the music of the
16th century, of the 12th or the 9th, and still less that
of the old Greeks, *really sounded*. We may be very
well informed, we may exercise the utmost care in
our researches and we may know what man can only
know today; still when we speak of ancient music, it
is as the blind man speaks of color. We lack the *living intuition* for it which is irretrievable, forever
lost.

So we see how difficult it is to discuss the history of
music. In painting, in sculpture and in architecture
the objects themselves are before us in indisputable
reality; in poetry we have written documents. In
music we have only a notation which offers liberal
opportunity for arbitrary interpretation. Even the instruments we use today are not over two or three hundred years old, some considerably younger. We know
of their immediate predecessors, but they are no

longer familiar to us and already sound strange. The farther we penetrate into the past the less we know what were the technical requirements for the execution of music. Even if we had an adequate notation, we would not know what to do with it because we lack the knowledge which in its time was taken for granted. It is as though I were to put a Wagner score before a person living in the 13th century; even though I were to explain all the indications carefully, he would not be able to visualise the whole because he would lack the intuitive understanding of the music. And as the man of the past would fare with the music of today, just so do we fare with the music of the past.

Let me try to make this clearer by a picture. Suppose we visited an old castle, famous for its fountains and cascades, like Versailles or Wilhelmshoehe. We see the plan, the structure of the terraces for the waterfalls, the network of pipes, the places where the fountains are meant to rise. Does that give us any idea of the effect of the whole? Scarcely, unless we see tall shafts of water spout up where the dull apertures of pipes had stared at us, or swift streams rushing over the bare terrace steps; unless, in other words, all this lifeless framework should suddenly burst into activity. But if the water has dried up, the pipes are choked and only a few fragments of this once great structure remain visible, then we may indeed see that an imposing project had once been here, but how it functioned and with what effects we can only guess.

This picture symbolises our relation towards the music of the past. What music we have in old manuscripts or know of through the findings of investigators covers a period of approximately 2500 years. Only the compositions of the last 250 years, or roughly a tenth of this time, are still accessible to us. For the rest, the living spring has gone dry, the pipes are choked, the grand stream of sound that once flowed through them is silenced. We may attempt to reconstruct it but we do not know how accurately our plan will correspond with the original.

I have tried to make very clear the difficulties of understanding music of the past, in order to show once more the error of regarding history as a developmental process. Since our picture of the past is but fragmentary and indistinct, we easily conclude that the past itself must have been imperfect, destined to unfold but gradually into perfection, a development being implied. It is like standing at the entrance to an avenue of poplars which extends as far as our eye can reach; the nearest trees will seem quite large, those a little farther off somewhat smaller, and those way back at the horizon like dots. Are they therefore in reality mere dots? Certainly not. If we walk along the avenue we find that the individual trees are different, one with a stronger trunk, another with richer foliage, but essentially they are all alike, and the last one, which looks like a dot, may well be bigger than the one we first stood next to. The cause of this illusion is not in the trees themselves but in the nature of our vision which shows us distances only in the foreshortening of perspective, a fact of which early plastic art was well aware, although it failed to use perspective, not because it was incapable of doing so, but because it would not admit the optical illusion.

The history of music is such an avenue of trees, along which we shall pass in the following pages. I have tried to show that we must constantly bear in mind the inadequacy of our vision, yet we need not for this reason assume that we cannot arrive at any understanding of the subject. Even where details are not clear, we know that a tree is always a tree, man always man, the musician always a musician, that the same initial forces operate in all these forms as are active within ourselves. Just because the musical past is so veiled in mystery, we cannot try too hard to grasp the warmth, the living human quality of what lies hidden in it. We must approach our subject through the comparative study of the varying phases of *human thought and feeling* by which music has always been conditioned. We must try to look upon history as if we lived it, as if we ourselves were the characters and took part in the events of which we speak; we shall then see them imbued with life, divulging more to us than all our searching among facts. For at best, these so-called facts are very uncertain notions. They are random fragments of a complex which could have real factual significance only as a whole, but which will never again appear in this entirety. We see only bits of the former reality, so that what today may count as fact and so serve as the basis for a broad theory of history, tomorrow may be found erroneous and completely overthrown by the discovery of new facts. Facts are aids to historical research but should be used with the utmost prudence; for, in truth, we never get beyond the stage of *hypothesis*.

Our hypothesis must be built not upon external facts, therefore, but upon the realization that art is conditioned by thought and feeling. This realization teaches us that art is art at all times, that it knows no ascent, climax or decline, no development, only unceasing transformation. This transformation is determined not by discoveries, so-called improvements in technique, or other influences from without. It is determined solely by the changes in man's capacity of perception. It is what we experience every day, every hour, every minute, within ourselves. It is the constant rearranging and transforming of forces which we call the process of life, and only so long as we change do we live.

Thus the history of music is to be seen as a moulding of human life in material ever so delicate, perishable, and elusive—the ringing, vibrating air which we call tone. We shall try to see it as the life story of tone, of the resonant forms of air, as the history of change in those perceptions by which men have grasped sound and moulded it into an art.

CHAPTER II

EARLY CHARACTERISTICS—THE GREEKS

WE have seen that the growth of form is not a development but a change in those perceptions by which the stuff of vibrating air is shaped into constantly new forms. The question now arises, what are the forces at work here which govern these changes in form?

If we survey the whole known course of music history in all countries, from the most ancient times to the present day, from exotic island nations to Western Europe, we find everywhere two great main categories: *cult* music and *secular* music. In this respect music is like architecture, which also develops a cult and a secular type in every style. Cult music usually serves the purposes of the church, although in ancient times it was used in the art of healing as well, when medicine was still linked with religious rites and the cult of magic. As long as the church has the power of holding the people to a common cult, that is, of satisfying their religious impulse by its doctrines, so long is cult music ecclesiastical. It is almost always so, but there are periods during which the power of the church relaxes and then we observe that

30

cult music—music, that is, which makes a universal popular appeal—inclines to become secular. We have just left such a period behind us, beginning in the 18th century with the so-called era of "the Enlightenment" and including the whole 19th century. During this time cult music turns away from the church and makes use of secular forms, to wit, the symphonies of Beethoven and Bruckner, the concert-masses of the 19th century, the spiritual music of Brahms and the operas of Richard Wagner—compositions which all show a mixture of the elements of cult and secular style—while actual church music decays and is employed merely for liturgical uses. But such periods are exceptional. They interrupt the normal course and are usually followed by more spiritual periods which bring forth a new spiritual cult music, indications of which, indeed, we may notice at present.

Thus cult music, one of the two great categories, derives its impulse mainly from spiritual needs. Its task is thereby circumscribed. It serves to express the solemn, the sublime, the mystical, artistic conceptions of the superhuman, the divine, the mysterious. The one important characteristic of music which differentiates it from all other arts, the invisibility of its form, is consciously used for the benefit of the cult.

Secular music, the other great category, is distinguished from cult music by the fact that it seeks not to preserve or increase the effect of the invisible, but rather to do away with it by associating itself with other more obvious forms of expression, easily perceptible to the senses. In this way the invisible is made clear by connection with something visible or definable; it is robbed of its incomprehensibility, it becomes secularised. This may be accomplished in different ways: first, through the combination of music with bodily movements, in the *dance;* secondly, through the combination of music with a poem, capable of existence without music, in the *song;* and thirdly, through the combination of music with both song and dance, the various forms of which are clearly coördinated and held together by a story. The last is the most artistic form of secular music, evolving later into the oratorio and the opera, forms which need not be discussed here save to realize their origin in song and dance. The dance and the song are the fundamental forms of all secular music, the essence of which always consists in clothing the invisibility of music with some other expression easily perceived by the eye or the reason, such as dance movements or the words of a song.

Having seen that musical forms originated at all times and in all countries in these two fundamental types—cult music, the servant and helpmate of the church, and secular music, the medium for the worldly dance and song—the question now urges itself upon us: what made people want to make music and how did they come upon this art? How was it possible to shape the invisible air into the likeness of music?

The answer would mean an inquiry into the origin of music which I do not intend to follow up here. It involves prehistoric times, about which after all we can only guess, and does not belong in a historical survey which should deal only with times in which music has taken definite form. Music may have originated in natural love-calls, or in religious ceremonies, or from the observation of the effects of vocal sounds prolonged in varying pitch; but all these questions belong in a separate field of research and have nothing to do with the history of music as an art. Nor shall we discuss here the invention of the first instruments. It is most probable that man first sang and then began to imitate the sound of the voice by mechanical means. But the reverse procedure is also imaginable. Very early in his experience, long before music can be historically dealt with, man must have known that he could produce tone by blowing tube-shaped instruments, striking resonant surfaces, or plucking vibratile strings. As far back as we can think, we have to reckon with his ability to produce tone both by singing and by means of instruments, and as this ability still exists among most uncivilized peoples, we may assume that it is to be found everywhere within historic times.

Many are the ways in which air was fashioned into tone. The difficulty of the process may be measured when we observe that there is scarcely a tone to be found in nature which remains fixed at the same pitch. To sing a given tone is difficult and demands exact self control. A naturally sung tone rises and falls with stronger or weaker breath. But as in building stones must be cut and shaped with a certain similarity in order that they may be laid one on top of another, so must the natural material of tone be cut and moulded, as it were, to a certain likeness. Tone as it is made into the material of music is divested of its natural character and formed according to certain arbitrary laws; it is *stylised*. The natural sound of the human voice in singing, which is a sort of cry sliding over several tones, is modified into a single rigidly fixed tone to which is added at a strictly defined distance, a second fixed tone, and similarly a third, a fourth, a fifth, sometimes a sixth, seventh, and more. Thus the whole compass of sound, which in the beginning had been somewhat chaotic, is now divided up according to certain definite laws. This division of tones into exact relationships we call a *tone-system,* and the standardization of tone in the tone-system is the first step in the construction of an art of music.

The principle in this process is the same among all civilized peoples, but the execution—the number of tones used, their respective distances from each other, the way, in other words, in which the chaos of sound crystallizes into single tones—varies greatly. This diversity is not surprising if one considers that the human voice undoubtedly played the leading rôle in the beginnings of artistic culture. Singing was bound to vary among the different peoples on account of racial divergences in temperament and feeling, differences in climatic conditions and especially in *physiological* make-up and *language*. So we have a considerable number of tone-systems underlying an equal number of musical cultures. Not all, to be sure, have evinced the same germinating power or have been equally productive. It is well to remember, nevertheless, that our Western European tone-system, while very significant and marvellous in its way, is but one branch on the tree of musical culture.

It is not possible to compare here the various exotic tone-systems, as for example the Chinese, Siamese, Arabian, and others. How they differ from ours in type and origin I have indicated. They rest upon essentially different perceptions of the nature of tone, of the distances and relations between tones. I would like now to limit our subject to the consideration of Occidental, and particularly of *Western European* music. Here, too, we find some variations in detail, for even within one cultural zone a tone-system does not remain unaltered but, like other symbols of culture, is subject to changes in perception.

The tone-system of the Greeks, who, though an Eastern European people must be included here on account of their general cultural importance, differed

from that used during the first thousand years of the
Christian era; the later Middle Ages, then the Renaissance and Baroque periods, again organised totally
different systems, and at the present time changes are
once more taking place. All these systems, however,
are culturally one in that they are all constructed of
whole and half tones and all based on the conception
of the octave as the unit of measurement. They differ
in many details, especially in the disposition of the
whole and half tones, that is, in the formation of
tonalities. The Greeks, as the people nearest to the
Orient, even made use of quarter tones. But these
differences are secondary to the main distribution of
sounds into whole-tones chiefly and a few half-tones,
and the limiting of the series at the octave. The
enigmatical similarity in sound between the first tone
and its octave, which lies five whole and two half
tones distant from it, is probably due to the perception of an acoustic law. If a string stretched between
two bridges is divided exactly in the middle by a third
bridge, each half will give the octave of the original
tone. Our sense of the octave, therefore, corresponds
to a sense of symmetry or proportion.

I have said that the tone-system of the Greeks
differs somewhat from our own, and this undoubtedly
holds good of their entire music. If we usually begin
the history of Occidental music with the Greeks, it
is more from a sense of moral obligation toward Greek
culture than because the influence of Greek music

itself was particularly strong. Indeed we can say little about its influence because we have but a very incomplete idea of Greek music as a whole. It would be untrue to say that we know nothing about it. We do know a good deal. We know that it played an important rôle in education, worship, drama, in the whole public life, that its significance was the subject of thorough philosophical investigation, from which an extensive theoretical literature of æsthetics developed which was influential well into the Christian era. We know that Greek music underwent several great changes in style, occasioned partly by the invasion of Greek culture by Asiatic elements. These Asiatic influences apparently brought instrumental music into greater prominence, causing a growth in individual virtuosity, generally speaking, and a strengthening of secular music as against the older cult music. This secularisation was looked upon as a form of weakness and aroused a violent opposition which echoes through the dialogues of Plato. I shall pass over the musical forms developed particularly in Greek worship and Greek tragedy. What I emphasised in the introductory chapter holds true here: that in spite of a fairly extensive knowledge of details, we cannot possibly imagine how this music *sounded*. Several pieces of Greek music have been preserved, deciphered and transcribed into a more modern notation; but even these transcriptions seem dead to us, mummified material fit for museums. The insurmountable difficulty in the way of our understanding Greek music lies in the fact that this music was essentially bound up with the *language* and received plastic form only through the living spoken word.

We may study an ancient language, learn its grammar and approximately fathom the logic of its thought, but the inner meaning—the undefinable sensation of rhythm, of cadence, of tempo—in short, the sound of the language, its very *soul*, remains closed to us. It is the possession of ancient man alone and has been buried with him. We differ from him in all respects because our perceptions and our attitude towards life have changed. Now it is precisely upon the feeling of the Greeks for their language that Greek music was based. It was not music as such, not an art. As the Greeks thought of themselves not as individuals but as members of a community whose lives centered in their common interest, the city-state, so their music was but a part of their language, their education, their community life, their culture. We understand enough to reconstruct but the skeleton of its original form. We know that the Greeks had a number of scales, each of which had its own character or *ethos*. We know that they disposed the tones not as we do, from below upwards, but from above downwards. We know that the Greeks did not possess harmonic music in our sense, but sang in unison or in octaves, the parallel voices apparently being freely embellished vocally or instrumentally.

We know that the Greeks did not have a musical rhythm in our sense, but gave their song a metric form in compliance with the laws of their language, to the latent music of which such treatment was particularly suited. We know here or there a theoretical detail, but the most important thing of all we do not know: namely, how this music really *sounded*.

Greek music is a beautiful myth of a world that has been. Its great influence upon succeeding times consists less in handing on actual musical examples than in stimulating ever anew the desire to reconstruct something that probably never existed in that particular form. For many efforts have been made —ever since the days of the Renaissance, of the Florentine opera and French tragedy, of Gluck's operatic reforms, of Schiller's "Bride of Messina" and Wagner's "Studies in Music"—to reconstruct antique drama with its peculiar relation to music. The Greek theorists also exercised a profound influence on the earlier Middle Ages. It is probably safe to say that all these efforts were based on mistaken ideas about Greek music, but the misunderstandings led to great productive results. We may therefore conclude, with all deference to research, that the true historic value of Greek music lies in the myth it has created about itself. The creation of this myth, which for centuries had a fructifying influence, was its greatest achievement.

CHAPTER III

GREGORIAN MUSIC—FIRST TO TENTH CENTURIES

GREEK music, in creating this myth about itself, became an inexhaustible source of inspiration to the theorist of early Christian times and to the creative artist from the later Christian era to the present. The less people knew about it the higher rose its prestige. That what they did know of it could be so soon forgotten was an inevitable consequence of the organic relation of Greek music to the Greek language. In the same measure that the language lost its inner vitality, the music was doomed to oblivion. The language was the tree on which music was in truth but the blossom.

Of the history of music during the great period of change marked by the growth of the Roman empire and the rise and spread of Christianity, we can, as in the case of Greek music, assert but little accurately. We know that the Romans were not a musical people; they imported their artists from Greece. Thus Greek music was transplanted to Rome, principally the more appealing instrumental music. Already strongly permeated with Asiatic elements in its home land, it

lost still more of its Greek character amid the con-
glomeration of cultures in Rome. We must bear in
mind that at that time Rome was as important eco-
nomically and politically as England in the 18th and
19th centuries and America in the 20th. Artists
ambitious for a wide success and large earnings
naturally sought the metropolis of the world. They
could scarcely be called bearers of culture, however,
since the taste of those who buy their art is apt to
demand entertainment after its own kind. Thus Greek
singers, dancers, sculptors, musicians, migrated to
Rome to find audiences, patrons and money, adapting
their performances to meet the wishes of pampered
but unimaginative connoisseurs.

Simultaneously there came to Rome another form
of art, less complaisant. The Christian communi-
ties which spread from Asia Minor through Greece
into Italy, employed a form of singing in which a
new cult music came into being, which originated
probably without any *artistic* intention and was for
that the more pregnant and profound in its effect. Of
the origin of this music we know nothing definite. It
may be connected with the Hebrew worship or traced
back to Greek or other influences. The probability is
that it sprang from several sources, transforming the
stimuli thus acquired into something new in accord
with the changed conditions. The impulse towards
musical reform came at first from the new worship
which in its very contrast to the earlier cult demanded

other artistic forms. But the deeper need of change emanated from that which had first given the old cult music life, *the language.*

I repeat, we cannot sufficiently beware of looking at the music of that time as a thing in itself. When we think of music today, we think involuntarily of music for its own sake, as a concert, the performance of a symphony or chamber music. But this kind of music only came about with the shaping of modern life. To men of ancient times music was conceivable only in connection with some event, whether worship, dance or recitation of poetry. *The word* was the most powerful influence in giving such music form. I have already pointed to the importance of tone-systems as preliminaries to a musical art. This means not that people constructed tone-systems and then began to make music with them, but that the artistic use of sound only begins when its fundamentals are defined by a tone-system, just as the artistic treatment of language is possible only when it has attained a reasonable vocabulary, logically connected to express thought. I have compared the formation of the tone-system with the simple laws by which a stone-cutter trims stones in order to build with them. But to achieve a building there must always be two things: first the building *material,* and secondly the building *idea.* These do not oppose, but are conditioned by, each other. The idea of building presupposes knowledge of the organic possibilities of

the material; it is the result of the productive interaction of material laws with the creative impulse of
human imagination. Now the medium which led ancient peoples to the discovery of laws in musical
material was *language*, that is, the feeling for the
spoken word.

This explains why ancient musical forms were
originally based upon the feeling for the rhythmic
quality of language and upon the physiological conditions of speech. So we see why Greek music *had* to
disappear leaving scarcely a trace when transplanted
to Western Europe. Furthermore we may understand
the peculiar picture presented today by the music
of the first ten centuries of the Christian era. For
all that has come down to us from this long period
is some *church* music. But the simplest reflection
tells us that people have always danced and sung;
they have never devoted themselves exclusively to
prayer, but, though things might be going ever so
badly with them, they have held their festivals and
made merry. Profane music *must* always have existed
alongside of cult music. That we know little or nothing about it, is due partly to the fact that nobody
took the trouble to write it down; also partly to the
fact that many secular compositions were undoubtedly taken over by the church in altered and purified
form. Nor must we forget that the contrast between
church and folk life was not as marked formerly as
it is today. Until the later Middle Ages the church

was the public gathering place where people not only prayed, but met, gossiped, did business and exchanged news. Religious paintings even as late as the 15th and 16th centuries represent such *genre* scenes in every variety. This importance of the church as a general gathering place and center of daily life had probably been greater, rather than less, in earlier centuries. So the *music* of the church may have met the *general* demand for music to the widest extent, leaving a comparatively narrow field for secular music.

But though these circumstances may appear to explain the predominance of cult music and our ignorance of secular music, the proper explanation, after all, is to be found in what we have said about *language*. I have pointed out dance and song as the fundamental types of secular music. Dance and song, in so far as they represent forms of art, are forms of *national* culture; they presuppose a characteristic national language. The culture of the first ten centuries after Christ, however, was not a national culture but a *church* culture; the languages of the time were not national languages, for there was really only one language—the Latin of the church. Therefore there could be only *one* art music—the church music connected with this church language.

Even in those days, of course, there were races, peoples, national types, but in spite of their differences they felt themselves members of the one big family whose head and center was the church. The church was their uniting spiritual bond; she gave them not only their religion, but education, learning, language, art. This universality was part of the temporal power of the church; and not until this power decayed with the fall of the house of Hohenstaufen was the soil ready for the growth of a national art. Or to put it the other way about, when a process of national division had begun in the intellectual and social structure of Central Europe, the temporal imperialism of the church, which represented a superficial cultural unity, was bound to decay first, to be followed several centuries later by the fall of the spiritual power with all its consequences. The historical process we observe here is one of increasing individualization of the nations and upon it the independent existence of secular music as an art hangs, for all secular music is national and presupposes a national language. If the language lacks cultural significance, the music will not survive; it disappears not because circumstances have changed but because it has no durability in itself. This holds true for the secular music of the first ten centuries after Christ. The real art music of this period is a *universal* music, founded upon the language of the church which was then the sole language of culture.

If, therefore, we want to get a vivid idea of the character of this universal music, we must keep the character of the language in mind. Now there appears a strange difference in language as it took shape

in western and in eastern countries, a difference which
I may only indicate here, but which was fundamental
in the upbuilding of western music. For, while the
oriental languages are essentially *metrical* languages,
that is, based on the proportionate length of syllables,
the occidental languages are based on *accent*, that is,
articulated according to the feeling for emphasis.
This results in an essentially different principle of
tone-formation in music. As it takes form, tone,
being affected chiefly by accent, must now free itself
from the language metre which is no longer the determining characteristic of language, and strive to
create an independent metre of its own. In this way
a syllable may be invested and amplified with rich
and ornamental melody without disturbing the language. Rather, the speech accent is thrown into
greater prominence when thus expanded through the
characteristic medium of music, converted, that is,
into tone having duration in time. The importance of
this process lies in the fact that music thus gradually
attains its own metre, independent of language, so
that while we are no more familiar with the music of
this period than with Greek music, we can more
easily imagine what it was like. Thus the less musical
language of the Occident, less rich in sound than that
of the Orient, leads to the creation of a more vital
and enduring world of tone.

There is a second factor which contributes to this
change in the structure of music. Greek music was

subject, through the metrical articulation of the language to which it was bound, to rational, concrete
laws of form, while western music, striving away
from the language metre, was not open to such concrete definition. We see here the contrast between
the whole ancient and Christian conceptions of life,
which manifests itself in music as in the plastic arts.
The common factor in Greek music and the music
of the first ten Christian centuries is their connection
with language. In the way in which they relate music
and language lies the great difference between them,
which may be just as well explained on purely
physiological grounds as on those of cultural psychology.

When I speak of the music of the first ten centuries A. D. as a unit, I am well aware of committing
no less a violence than if I talked of music from the
10th to the 20th centuries as a whole. But I have
said before that we *know* very little, and that even
this little is disputed. So that either we repair with our
subject to the battle-ground of philological discussion, or we endeavor to grasp its artistic significance.
A thousand years is naturally a period of manifold
achievements and revolutions in art, but a few of the
main outlines are still visible and these alone I shall
attempt to indicate.

The general characteristic of music from the first
until about the 10th century is that, like Greek music,
it moved in *unison*. Not that harmonisation was not

understood. This music neither needed nor was at all capable of harmonisation, nor did it progress in measured time and rhythmic periods but moved, to our way of thinking, in free recitation. The biblical psalms were first taken as texts since they were suited to antiphonal singing, and later on hymns inspired composition. Some of these hymns of the 4th and 5th centuries have come down in altered form in the late Protestant chorale—the old *Veni Redemptor Gentium,* for instance, which became the chorale "Savior of the Heathen Known." In our own day the text of the 9th century Pentecostal hymn *Veni Creator Spiritus* has been made use of by Mahler in his eighth symphony.

Of the creative *personalities* of these centuries we know only by legend. The two names of greatest significance are those not of composers but of princes of the church, in whose times and under whose leadership important events took place or at least had their inception. They are those of *Ambrosius,* Bishop of Milan about 390, and Pope *Gregory the Great,* who lived two hundred years later. From Ambrosius dates the systematic introduction of congregational singing in the form of hymns for double chorus, the tendency, in a measure, toward secularization, toward popularization and the participation of the laity in music. The Gregorian reforms opposed this tendency but not in a sense hostile to music. Gathering the entire treasure of ecclesiastical music into a magnificent liturgical system, Gregory legitimized music as an independent and important part of worship by definite legislation. Schools for singers had existed in Rome proper since about the 4th century, to which new ones were now added in Italy and later on in the neighboring countries to the north. To these schools fell the task of carrying through the whole domain of the Roman church the art of ritualistic singing prescribed by Gregory, so that music became uniformly obligatory in the celebration of the mass and in all church rites, and was everywhere performed in the same manner.

Gregorian plain-song, an achievement of the first rank not only in music but in general culture, is the great contribution of the first ten centuries of Christendom. Church music thereafter grew with some variation in detail but without fundamental change. The establishment and systematic spread of this sacred art was the farthest-reaching achievement of the church in behalf of music. It provided music with a universal form suited to occidental conceptions, which now, supported by the mighty authority of the church, swept on from south to north finding new patronage and inspiration in the monasteries, the great centers of culture in the Northern countries (especially Metz in France and St. Gall in German Switzerland) where it was further cultivated, altered, and enriched. Then, after the turn of the 10th century, as the nations begin to realize their individuality, the contacts of Gregorian art with Italian, German and French elements bring about further changes in musical form.

CHAPTER IV

POLYPHONY, A NEW ART—TENTH TO FOURTEENTH CENTURIES

THE Gregorian chant, which we regard as the foundation of music after the 6th century, was not only a certain type of song, but over and above all, a great and far-reaching musical *style*. Considerable variation occurs within any style in the course of centuries, although the fundamental features are retained, and this also happened with Gregorian plain-song. The most important factor in bringing about these changes was perhaps, as I have suggested, its transplantation into different countries and the influence upon its practice of national characteristics. Though we may suppose that the Roman form was at first faithfully handed on, still the monks who took it up were in one country Italian, in another German, in others French and English. Differences in national temperament, in language, in climatic conditions, in disposition for singing and in imaginative trend— all these together must have undesignedly wrought changes which in the course of centuries amounted to variations of some moment.

It was impossible, moreover, to check the manner of singing accurately, since notation with exact directions for pitch and time did not exist. Verbal traditions were relied on principally, while the so-called *neumes* served to aid the memory. I have already pointed out that these neumes were a sort of sound-stenography, a graphic representation of sound-movements, in which certain symbols, like the dash and dot, indicated duration. I have also mentioned the fact that neume writing was not uniform but varied in different times and among different peoples, some of its forms remaining undeciphered to this day. But here again it would be wrong to imply imperfection in bygone times and to point with pride to our perfected notation. It is more correct to say that our conception of exactness was foreign to the people of that time, and, had they known it, would probably not have met with their approval. We should, indeed, think of the old way of making music as freer than ours and, with all its strict discipline, partaking more of the nature of improvisation. These people of the Middle Ages were men of much more imagination than we are now. Because from the start they took for granted a certain intellectual uniformity created by the church, they could indulge individual fancy more freely. This is to be seen as much in their free treatment of architectural detail or in their inventive carving of choir-benches as in their music.

Let us therefore refrain from defining the gradual

metamorphosis of neumes into a notation similar to our own as "progress." It was merely a change that met new exigencies. By the end of the 10th century it had become customary to add a second voice to unison singing. What this custom should be traced back to, it is difficult to say. It might be explained naturalistically on the grounds that western voices, especially among the Nordic types, are by nature sharply divided into high and low, and that two such different voices tend to sing together not in unison nor in octaves, but in keeping with the natural distance between them, approximately in fifths. This tendency must have been the more pronounced the less cultivated the voices were, that is, the farther the singers were from Rome. As a matter of fact, we must look for the beginnings of polyphonic music not in the South but in the North, to wit, in England and France.

Let me emphasize that this suggested explanation based on the natural differences in voices especially noticeable in the North, is only a hypothesis among others. Whatever its origin, the appearance of two-voiced singing is the first indication of that form which has distinguished occidental music among all the music cultures of the world, namely *polyphony*. It is this polyphonic tendency which gradually penetrates the great style of the Gregorian chant and brings about a new musical form.

We must picture this growth of part singing as

happening in several stages. First, two voices sang the same words and the same series of tones but in different pitch. They moved in *fourths* or *fifths*. Even today one may often notice that two musical but untrained people sing together in parallel fifths. In England accompaniment in sixths and thirds instead of fifths seems to have appeared early. These are the natural types of two-voice singing. Somewhat more ingenious, more intellectual, is the idea of counter-motion, where the second voice descends while the first rises and vice versa. To the second voice, which in principle is not the lower but the upper voice, a third may be added, which goes in octaves with the first, and to this again a fourth voice may be added. The text and the length of the notes are at first the same in all the voices, but here, too, changes grad-ually set in. The accompanying voice becomes inde-pendent, breaking its rigid attachment to the first, achieving its own melodic features and finally also its own text.

These are roughly the lines along which sacred music moved in different countries from about the 9th to the 13th century. Music of this sort was bound to need a different kind of notation, for the neumes which presupposed unison singing were inadequate to the polyphonic style. It was now necessary that nota-tion should definitely indicate first the *pitch*, so as to make clear the distances between the voices, and secondly the *duration* of tones, so that the voices

GUITTONE   D'AREZZO
NACQUE IN SUBBIANO NEL CONTADO ARETINO. E INCERTO L'ANNO
DEI SUOI NATALI. FU ASCRITTO ALL'ORD DEI CAV. CHIAMATI FRATI
GAUDENTI. FONDO E DOTO IL MONASTERO DEGLI ANGIOLI DI FI
RENZE. MORI NEL 1294. LE DI LUI OPERE CONTENGONO POESIE E LET
MA LE PR. NON SI RAMMENTANO LE 2. SONO IN PREGIO PRESSO I COLTIVATORI
DELLA LINGUA ITALIANA

could be held together even though they moved in independent rhythm.

The first requirement led to the invention of the *staff*. At first one line was drawn, and later several lines, each designating a certain pitch, and the neumes were placed on the corresponding line. This idea appeared in several places, but the four-line staff, which came to be of fundamental importance, was the invention of the Italian monk, *Guido of Arezzo,* who lived about the year 1000. He is generally considered the greatest teacher and pedagogue of this time and the following, and it need not concern us here whether the reforms attributed to him really originated with him or are only included under his name.

To these reforms, beside the staff in which pitch was distinguished by different colored lines, belongs also the division of the customary tone-system of twenty tones into so-called *hexachords,* scales of six steps, having a half tone between the third and fourth steps. This classification, beside which the original octave grouping still held, was intended mainly for the teaching of singing. Each tone was sung on the first syllable of a different line of a certain Latin hymn:

"*Ut* queant laxis
*Re*sonare fibris
*Mi*ra gestorum
*Fa*muli tuorum

*So*lve polluti
*La*bii reatum,
  Sancte Johannes."

These are the so-called *solmisation* syllables which are still used in all Latin countries. The syllables represented not specific tones, for which Gregory had already introduced the letters of the Latin alphabet, but their positions in the hexachord. The names remained the same throughout all the hexachords, so that when several hexachords were combined the syllables had to be interchanged in the process of singing. This interchange, which naturally required keen attention and an ability to transpose quickly, was called *mutation*.

Thus, in brief, we see that the teaching of music meant simply the teaching of *singing*, with which, indeed, the whole theory of music during this period was solely concerned. The living voice was the material to be fashioned, and music only existed, so to speak, to give the voice opportunities for expression. We possess a great many theoretical writings, dating from the close of the 10th century, by learned monks who indulge in all sorts of speculations. We are apt to forget that these were meant to be rules not for composing but for singing. What we call composition, individual artistic creation for its own sake, the expression of personality, was as yet entirely unknown. People wanted to hear singing, and the composer was less a creator than a master and teacher of singing.

The new polyphonic singing, as we have seen, required that the pitch and the duration of tones should be fixed in the notation. Guido's method offered the proper basis for fixing the pitch. But to express duration a new method was to be gradually worked out. The characters were now given a common form, to which special signs were added indicating the duration of each tone in relation to the rest. A system of comparative fractions was thus introduced into notation; tones were measured by their relative duration. Hence we now speak of a *mensural* or measured music. Music develops its own rhythm, independent of the language metre and divisible into mathematical relations, which are expressed in the notation.

These achievements in defining pitch and duration are still apparent in the musical notation of today. We must remember that the conception of the duration of sound is always relative. I may say the comparative duration of two tones shall be as one to two, that is, the second shall sound twice as long as the first; but this only defines a proportion, and it is left to me how long I hold the first note, so long as the second has double its length. This relativity which determines merely the proportion and not the actual length of tones is still peculiar to the notation of the present day, for proportion may be rationally determined, but the underlying concept of time is not subject to such determination.

I shall not recount here the names of well known theorists and composers of this period. It is significant that more theory has come down or at least is known to us, than music. But we must beware of accepting the statements of the theorists as absolutely reliable descriptions of the practice of the time—that would be unfair to both their time and ours. It has probably always been true of art that rules and concepts are first theoretically formulated only when practice has already moved on to other rules for which no theoretical formula has yet been established.

The tendency towards polyphonic development which I spoke of as characteristic of music from about the 9th to the 13th century, first appeared in the Northern countries, and here it was most effectively carried on. About this time we are again very scantily informed. An endless amount of material must have been lost, a good deal may be still undiscovered, some is known but not yet accessible, and but little is actually available. England and northern France in particular seem to have come forward in the 12th and 13th centuries with important and characteristic contributions to the realm of polyphonic church music. About the English music we have little information, and that mostly indirect. In France, the masters of the Notre Dame School in Paris exercised an important leadership for several generations. They especially cultivated the type of polyphony sketched above, the joining of a number of voices, independent melodically, rhythmically and in text, in the so-called *motet*. Not that elsewhere, in Italy, in Germany, in Spain, the pursuit of music had ceased. But we observe that in any given period of artistic productivity certain places, for one reason or another, tend to stand out as centres of intensity, where the general activity is carried on with special vigor and success. Perhaps the lack of natural beauty in the voices of Northern peoples acted as an inducement to developing the charm of combined voices. Productive forces, too, must have been extraordinarily vigorous in the France of the 12th and 13th centuries, as is also shown by the architecture of the period.

Added to all this, there was a rich source of artistic inspiration in *national poetry* which now came definitely to the fore. Through it secular music came into its own and this in turn stimulated church music. The day of chivalric poetry began—in Germany the *minnesingers*, in France the Provençal *troubadours* and northern *trouvères*—and with it began a secular art music which, based upon the dance and the strophic song, was ennobled by contact with the more serious music of the church, while it in turn imbued the latter with a new sentience for words, for rhythm, for ideas. From the history of literature we know that in Germany this gallant art of singing and poetizing was later carried on in the middle-class society of the mastersingers, whose originality apparently lay rather on the poetical than on the musical side. We know less about the music than about the poetry of the older minnesingers, whereas the music of the trouvères has been preserved in large measure. Whether this fact enables us to judge of the actual musical productivity of the different countries, is not for us to consider. The most noteworthy musical events in German-speaking territory still occurred in the monasteries. Even here, with the development of the Christmas and Easter and other biblical plays, the music of the church became secularized, certain melodies were sung to texts in the vulgar tongue. But no such great art came from either Germany or Italy as the French music of the 12th and 13th centuries, both sacred and profane. Italy first began in the course of the 14th century to produce similar notable compositions of her own. There were also secular compositions, partly polyphonic, partly homophonic, but with the accompaniment of instruments. The term homophony in this case means only the standing out of a single voice against the others and does not imply harmonization of a melody in the modern sense.

Of this music, cultivated in Italy in the form of the madrigal, the *ballata* and the *caccia* (dance and hunting songs) we also know little. It was collectively called *Ars Nova*, after the title of a manuscript which appeared in France about the year 1350, just as the Florentines of 1600 spoke of a *nuova musica,* and we today speak of "modern music." The novelty of this *Ars Nova* lay primarily in the intensive saturation of sacred music with elements of secular origin, in the occasional subordination of accompanying voices to a leading voice, in the freer melodic and rhythmic treatment of the parts, in the frequent use of instruments to accompany the voice. These changes necessitated in turn a more flexible and diversified sort of notation. They can all be traced to the invasion of the universal cult form by national elements, to the liberation of music from the Latin of the church and its organic amalgamation with national languages. The process corresponds to an increasing secularization of things ecclesiastical in general, as expressed in other fields of culture. But over and above all these reforms, it is the human voice in its supremacy which still remains the real dictator of musical form. All the music of this time is primarily *vocal* music, and its forms spring from the urge to give the voice expression. This is true also of the great compositions which the 15th and 16th centuries now bring to light.

CHAPTER V

THE NETHERLANDS

THE period we now approach, which includes roughly the 15th and 16th centuries, stands out in relief against preceding times on account of its great variety of musical activities and the number of composers who seem to appear suddenly upon the scene. Individuality becomes more noticeable, the fortunes of the different composers command attention, and the observer might easily be led to believe that music, having passed through its elementary schooling in essentials during the first 1300 years of the Christian era, now begins to be a real art. I warned the reader against such an impression in the introductory chapter and would now like to repeat the warning.

In the 19th century it was good form to speak of the Middle Ages as the "Dark Ages." Meanwhile we have realized that the weakness of our sight by no means implies darkness of the object seen, and that these supposedly dark Middle Ages were sometimes brighter than our own times. The intellectual and artistic achievement of the Middle Ages, early and late, and of the times which preceded them, deserve our highest esteem, and we must beware of applying

64

the term "primitive" to them in a derogatory sense. The Gregorian chant is not at all primitive, but can only be regarded as a great, far-reaching and inherently rich artistic and cultural expression. The same is true of early polyphonic music, the great French compositions of the 12th and 13th centuries, the secular music of national lyric character, and the *Ars Nova*. If we now see little but the general outlines of it all, yet we may assume that where such outlines are still visible through the centuries, there must really have been an extraordinary wealth of musical activity.

If music history after the 15th century seems clearer to us, it is not that there is now more music to deal with, but that we can understand it better. Not alone because we are closer to this period in time. The plastic art of the Greeks and Egyptians is thousands of years older than early Christian music, yet it is more familiar to us. The difficulty in an historical evaluation of music always lies in the inadequacy of transmission and particularly in our unfamiliarity with the tone perceptions of former times.

On this account I keep reminding the reader that the material of music is resonant, vibrating air—tone. The block of marble the sculptor hewed five thousand years ago retains its original form. But the ringing air, which the composer only five hundred years ago moulded after certain rules into a pattern of tones, blows away, while an intelligent understanding of the note picture that is left—which, though unquestionably faithful, gives us merely a relative idea of the form of the music—is bound up with many assumptions which we have lost sight of.

Now as regards the tone-perception upon which it was based, music from the 15th century on, stands somewhat nearer to us than that which preceded it, and this is the chief reason—beside the fact that documents are better preserved and more legible—why we are able to speak with greater certainty about it. I repeat, it is *somewhat* nearer to us, we are better able, perhaps, to get an approximate idea of it. This music is still so extraordinarily different from ours that to many present-day musicians it seems absolutely dead.

The period preceding the 15th century was characterized, as I have said, by the invasion of western European music, which had originated everywhere as cult music, by *national* impulses—the polyphony which came from the northern countries, the secularizing of form brought about by a dawning national poetry, the blossoming of a secular art-music, and also the introduction of instruments. All these factors had naturally influenced sacred music, corresponding to a certain secularization of the church which now became noticeable in other fields as well. The Papacy, we should remember, had launched its great battles for world supremacy. The removal of the Pope's residence from Rome to Avignon at the beginning of the 14th century coincides significantly with the prominence at that time of French art in general and of French music in particular.

During the period which now follows the situation is reversed. National secular music, to be sure, still exists and leads in the different countries—France, Italy, Germany, England—to further alterations in the fundamental types of dance and song. But over and above this, a strong unifying tendency is noticeable anew in sacred music, which eventually embraces all separate national currents and amalgamates them in one great art of universal importance. Cult music had refreshed and enriched itself with the folk-spirit of the different nations; it now takes over this wealth of folk-material and all the new incentives that come with it, and combines it once more with the solemn form of the liturgy. The rôle of music in the liturgy remains as Gregory had defined it. But the music itself has changed. It is no longer the unisonous plain-song of the Gregorian order. It is a choir of many voices for which the old Gregorian melodies and also the more recent folksongs may serve as a nucleus, a choir still designed for pure song, but in which the voices now intermingle with a freedom heretofore unknown. Each voice sings independently and yet is organically related to all the others.

This period is called the period of *polyphonic* music. The centre of musical intensity moves slowly from France towards the neighboring Netherlands, but does not remain localized there. The composers of the Netherlands begin to wander; they penetrate as far down as Italy, becoming the Pope's chapel singers or journeying to Venice, and they also settle in southern Germany. Now, and now only, through the influence of the Netherland teachers in Rome and Venice and in Munich, do these two great countries, Italy and Germany, enter upon the era of their own creative activity in music.

It is scarcely necessary to remind the reader that the striking prominence of the Netherland composers from about 1400 to 1600 finds a counterpart in painting and art as a whole in their country, and that all this activity goes hand in hand with the political power of the Netherlands at the time. These two-hundred years are in fact collectively spoken of in music as the period of the *Netherlands*. If we stop to consider what two-hundred years mean in art, we shall realize that this generalization must assume a great many individual variations. It is correct enough to sum up the period from 1700 to 1900 briefly as the era of harmonic instrumental music, but in this way individual personalities like Bach, Haydn, Mozart, Wagner, Schumann, Brahms, Bruckner, are simply thrown into one, without more ado. Musical currents must have been just as various in the days of the Netherlands as they were in this later period.

We distinguish, in general, five great groups or

schools which are named after their leading masters. The first and oldest of these masters, *Dufay*, was born in 1400, the last and most influential for our own time, *Orlandus Lassus* (also called Roland Lassus, or Orlando di Lasso) died in 1594. These dates indicate approximately the extent of the period. Orlandus Lassus, who lived in Munich and thus reached over into the German sphere of culture, is a contemporary of the great Roman *Palestrina* and of the Venetians, *Gabrieli* and his nephew of the same name. His music thus already belongs to a period of dawning national distinctiveness. Between Dufay, the first, and Lassus, the last representative of the music of the Netherlands, the most important composers to be mentioned are *Okeghem* and *Obrecht*; in the following generation, *Josquin des Près*, whose importance for his time is similar to Mozart's for the last 150 years; and finally *Adrian Willaert*, the founder of the Venetian school. These are, of course, but a few names picked from an almost inconceivable number. It was the time of great self-governing cities and small principalities, each and all of which took an ambitious pride in cultivating the arts. Thus musical centres were formed everywhere, and the few names mentioned represent only the highest peaks of a mighty mountain range. Nor would it be fair to assume that all musicians were necessarily Netherlanders. The music of the Netherlands was at first closely related to French and also to English music, but in the course

of its development more and more German and Italian
elements mingled with it as well, so that it now exercised a certain unifying influence. Up to the beginning of the 16th century the greatest masters were
indeed of Netherlands descent. They were not local
figures, however, but world-citizens of the great
realm of universal culture.

Now it is my intention not to dwell upon the differences in style of the Netherland schools or the
particular characteristics of their leaders, but rather,
after pointing out that these differences did exist in
a period of almost two hundred years, to speak of the
music of the Netherlands as a whole, omitting, for the
moment, the later part of the period, that of Orlandus
Lassus. It is permissible to treat the subject thus inclusively because all the masters of this time work
with the same material, namely the *human voice,* and
furthermore they treat this material, though each in
his own way, on the same principles, namely *poly-
phonically,* in many parts. They all speak the same
language, but with the varied shading of different
dialects and with an increasing number of words.

This great music has often been unjustly called dry
and technical, an artificial manipulation of tone, a
scholastic sophistry, and not considered as an art but
dismissed as "science." Simple reflection tells us that a
period which achieved such greatness in other fields of
art as the 15th and 16th centuries achieved would
hardly have been content with a dry and learned

music, and would still less have highly honored the masters who produced it. The source of this error is clear. People have been accustomed to judging the music of the Netherlands on paper, instead of realizing that music itself lies not in the written note but in the living sound. In this case the sound is that of the human voice. Only in understanding the nature of the voice do we find the key to the music of the Netherlands.

As pictured in notes, this music does at first seem like a problem in arithmetic. It is built on the type of polyphonic phrase known as counterpoint—in the original meaning of *punctus contra punctum,* note against note. A note in one voice corresponds to a note in another voice. The leading of the voices is mathematically regulated, so that the second voice, let us say, sings exactly the same tones as the first but starting one measure later; and after another measure a third voice follows and finally a fourth. Or the second voice sings the same series of tones as the first but twice as fast or twice as slowly, while the third voice moves in some other proportionate relation. Or the voices are so put together that one is the same as the other if read backwards; or they are led in counter-motion, that is, when the first moves up a third the second moves down a third, and so on. The possibilities of contrapuntal invention are here but briefly indicated. The masters who discovered these combinations showed imagination indeed, and a joy in technical craftsmanship which did not shrink from the difficult or the unusual.

Taking these compositions from the picture the notation gives of their carefully ordered construction, it may indeed seem as if one had to deal with a purely mathematical problem in which tones have been substituted for numbers. The impression is entirely different if one considers them not from the notation, which is never more than a makeshift, but from the character of the sound material out of which they were conceived. It is indeed very difficult for us, children of an age of instrumental music and harmonic tone-conception, really to understand music which conceived every tone in the character of the human voice and to which the consonance of tones laid one above another, as in our harmony, was absolutely unknown. It is difficult, but at least we must admit the difficulty and agree that the difference does exist.

The human voice is fundamentally different in nature from instrumental tone, and just as marble differs from brick, having different inherent possibilities of form and demanding different treatment, so the voice requires other forms than instrumental tone. The voice sings forth, unfolding itself in horizontal time-succession, and must be given form by the shaping of this continuous current of tone into rhythmic patterns. Upon the æsthetic sense and artistic arrangement of this rhythmic motion, which might even be described as the dance of tone, the charm of unison singing is based. If the first voice is joined by a second singing the same melody but entering later, as in the canon, two continuous movements are launched which really agree but the effect of which is intensified by the separate entrances and the constant following of one upon the other. I am not attempting to state a theory of æsthetics (the ideas touched upon here are discussed in my little pamphlet on "The Nature of Tone") but pointing out that the essential spirit of this polyphonic vocal music does not lie in the technical ingenuity of its forms at all, however remarkable they may appear. A principle is at work in the creation of these forms, a principle which causes the shaping of tone into continuous rhythmic patterns of marvellous complexity in their relationships. The mathematical laws underlying these relationships are no other than those which apply in the construction of a beautiful building. If the mathematical element appears particularly important in this music, we must not forget that the material of which it is made is the most impressionable stuff in existence—the warm breath of the human voice. In this way must we try to comprehend the nature and meaning of the music of the Netherlands. It is no mere technical jugglery and affectation, but one of the most vital and most ingenious productions of the human mind and the human imagination.

CHAPTER VI

POLYPHONIC AND HARMONIC MUSIC— SIXTEENTH CENTURY

WE have considered the music of the Netherlands— the contrapuntal, polyphonic vocal style—with regard both to its phrase form and to its tone material. The two at first seem incompatible, but in reality they complement each other. The phrase, consisting of the artistic combination of rhythmic patterns, is, as it were, purely mathematical in form. Its progress has nothing to do with emotion, all dynamic elements are left out of it; we seem to experience the pure play of numbers appearing as resonant time-relations. But it is the human voice which manifests them, and in order to convey music created, so to speak, out of the living body, this abstract mathematical form is necessary. For the voice is man *himself,* man in all his nakedness, projected from the visible into the invisible, the ringing air. The ear, by which we apprehend man as singing voice, gives us a much more sensitive impression of his being than the eye which sees but the actual body. So we can understand why a great art that makes use exclusively of the warm, sensitive material of the human voice is forced to the most abstract type of form in the moulding of it. It argues a misunderstanding of the nature of this music simply to analyse its form without considering the character of the material for which that form was meant. Here again, we see how necessary it is to consider any kind of music not as pictured in notes but as heard, as actual tone-sensation.

So far we have dealt with the first two-thirds only of the so-called period of the Netherland masters. During this time cult music, which had undergone secularisation and national partition, was at first united again in the church. But towards the end of this period a growing countermovement sets in which brings a decisive change for the 16th century. The great process of the redistribution of culture begins, which we call inclusively the *Reformation*. The Reformation was by no means an affair only of the church, the priests and the theologians. It was a tremendous process of fermentation in which social, national, economic and spiritual forces of a new sort came to the surface, finding their most powerful expression in the philosophical controversies of religious opinion. The Reformation was made not only by the so-called reformers—Luther, Zwingli, Calvin, and others. It was made by the Humanists also, the men of the Renaissance who turned back to the Greek ideal; by the man who established that the earth is round and moves around the sun; by the man who sailed over the unexplored ocean to get to India and thereby discovered America without knowing what he really had discovered; by the man who invented the art of printing; by the man who founded experimental physics, drew up its fundamental laws and initiated natural scientific research.

These things did not all happen at once, but were cumulative, one impelling another. We must picture the varied activity in all intellectual fields in order to understand its effect in political, economic and social matters, and to get an approximate idea of what really went on in the minds of the people of the time. Briefly, this was the birth of an entirely new world-picture, of the consciousness of forces, relations, possibilities which nobody had heretofore suspected. Fundamental ideas which had been held as eternal and unassailable truths, like the teachings of the Bible, were found to be untenable. Heretofore unimagined possibilities of exerting influence at a distance, as by the spreading of ideas in print, opened up intercourse to an incredible extent. Man saw himself surrounded by strange natural forces which he learned by scientific research to master and direct. He became conscious of the *physical aspect of the world*, the world as the sum of interactive elemental forces operating according to physical laws, and of his own physical nature. The fight against the church as the power which rigidly adhered to the old ideas was only the last expression of the struggle, variously waged in different countries, to achieve and establish this new world-picture.

To this new picture music, too, owes a change—the last and greatest change it has yet undergone—its transformation into *harmonic* music. It is naturally the process not of a year, nor of a decade or a century, but of several centuries. Nor is it a discovery, as discoveries cannot be made in art at all. It is the accompanying symptom of that great process of intellectual revolution which in church and political history is called the Reformation, and which in the history of thought is known as the era of physical science. A new sort of man is born; he controls invisible space and the forces thereof. He explores the laws governing the courses of the stars and the movements of the earth; he sails the waters of this earth to unknown continents; he observes the laws and forces of motion and space, of equilibrium and gravity, of magnetism and electricity. Thus in the plastic arts he works by the laws of dimension and perspective, and thus in music he creates the resonant column of air conceived in space which we call harmony, and the phenomenon of layers of tone conceived as a unit which we call the chord. The achievement of harmony comes with the great final period of the Netherlands, whose last great master, Orlandus Lassus, is also one of the first masters of harmonic music.

Until now I have never spoken of harmony but only of homophony or polyphony. Polyphony has nothing to do with harmony. We may have difficulty in thinking so, yet it is necessary to make this point clear. Polyphony is, as the name indicates, the combination of several voices. The independence of the single voice is fundamental; it has its own tonal character and exists for itself, always striving to make its individuality count. The art of polyphony consists in combining many such voices so that each retains its own character while their combined activity presents a well-ordered whole. This was the art of the Netherland masters which led them to the mathematically organized forms of counterpoint.

Harmony is not polyphony but *homophony*. When we hear the C major chord, we really hear only one tone, the C. We hear it not as a unit but divided into a plurality of tones, as if we looked at a point through a magnifying glass and saw it to consist of several separate points which to the naked eye look like one. We know today, which the people of that time did not know, that this dividing up, this refraction of a single tone into the several tones of a chord, corresponds to an acoustic law. There are really no single tones, for each tone is a compound of several tones of different vibrations, and the pitch and timbre of the principal tone are regulated by the relative number of its vibrations. The sounds which we perceive as harmony are the combination of the strongest vibrations in a tone; in other words, we apprehend a tone as the vertical compilation of its principal fractions. This physical phenomenon of overtones, like the refraction of light, was not known to the people of the 16th century; together with the law of harmonic relations, it was not scientifically established until about 1700. But although this law had not yet been scientifically recognized, it had been instinctively felt, because man's perceptions generally had taken this turn toward the physical. We thus observe in music what may also be seen in the other arts, and indeed in all aspects of life: namely, that people think and act in accord with new laws long before these laws have become exact knowledge. Scientific cognizance is always the last step in such a realisation.

Now it must not be understood from the foregoing that harmonic music in our sense was general in the 16th century. On the contrary, contrapuntal forms still prevailed and in music history this time is spoken of as the height of vocal polyphony. Actual history, however, like life itself, does not move in separate periods, the idea of which we subsequently introduce in order to bring events into some sort of order. Inevitably we sometimes carry our scheme too far and sections which for intrinsic reasons should already belong to a succeeding period are for superficial reasons credited to the preceding period. Certainly the 16th century still used mostly polyphonic forms and still conceived tone mainly as the sound of the human voice, and because its composers so clearly bring home to us the idea of vocal polyphonic music, we consider them the greatest masters of this style. But this very impression is due to the fact that in the works of these masters the *harmonic* sense of tone already plays a great part. Not only do they contain many purely harmonic phrases, but the treatment of the polyphonic style also, the independent contrapuntal voice-leading, is governed by harmonic concord, by considerations of consonance and dissonance, to a much greater extent than in the period preceding. Then we must not forget that even in this preceding period similar things were happening. For the history of art is not like a train travelling from station to station, stopping ten minutes here and twenty minutes there, but is an incessant movement within which the forces are constantly working, creating.

The peculiarity of the music of the 16th century is that it has, as it were, two faces, one turned forward, the other backward. Technique and form outwardly are of the past, but their treatment shows features which become decisive for the future. There is a well-known tale of how Palestrina rescued church music, which at the Council of Trent had been doomed to be discarded for its artificiality, by composing a new and simple piece in which he proved that art need not necessarily be complicated though it used all the resources of technique. No historical

proof of this incident is to be found, nor does anything in Palestrina's compositions indicate its probability, since long before this particular time he wrote
very simple works and at a later period exceedingly
artificial ones. The story is significant, nevertheless,
for it voices the sense of transition from music that
is primarily *polyphonic* to music that is once more
primarily *homophonic*. It is no longer the homophony of the Gregorian chorale, however, but that
of the multiple harmony of the chord.

Palestrina is justly considered the representative of
this period, which marks the end of the Middle Ages
in music and the commencement of the new harmonic
era. But to picture this time approximately we must
recall that during the very years when Palestrina was
working in Rome, the school founded in Venice by
Willaert of the Netherlands also flourished greatly and
was represented by two most important composers,
the *Gabrielis*. At this time, too, *Orlandus Lassus*, the
last of the great Netherlanders, was living in Munich.
Before that another Netherlander, *Heinrich Isaak*,
composer of one of the most beautiful chorales still
sung in Germany today, had been active in South
Germany and in Vienna. And finally, during approximately the same years, a new foundation for
musical culture was laid in northern Germany
through Luther's reforms. Luther still thought of
music as polyphonic, his great ideal being his contemporary, Josquin de Près of the Netherlands. But

through Luther's introduction of congregational singing and his adapting of the great spiritual folk-tunes
into the Protestant chorale, the tendency toward
homophony increased and polyphonic music was
forced into harmonic forms.

This diversity of musical activity, of which only
the outstanding examples are here mentioned, shows
how the unifying power of a single, universal catholic art, which had been influential for a time, again
splits up. But now the divisions are determined not
by language only, as before, but much more by the
local characteristics of religion. There is a Roman
catholicism, a Venetian catholicism, a South German
catholicism, a protestantism predominantly North
German, with offshoots in France, in England, in
Switzerland. All these forms of religion, which correspond with national characteristics, produce distinctive forms of religious music, at least in so far
as they are not fundamentally inimical to music.
Catholicism inclines to adhere to polyphony, to the
delight in many different voices singing together, although the single voice gradually loses its independence and becomes identified with the harmony. Protestantism at first also adheres to customary forms, but
it puts an end to the distinction between clergy and
laity, between choir and *congregation*. The congregation takes an active part, the language becomes that
of the people, and here too the polyphony of ingen-

iously woven voices gradually becomes the harmonically accompanied homophony of choral singing.

These things all come about in a variety of ways, very gradually and over wide stretches of time. Most significant is the development of the harmonic sense as the new way of hearing and feeling music. This is accompanied by the reciprocal interaction of cult and secular music. And with this comes the most important development of all, the awakening consciousness of an art of music wherein tone is produced by mechanical means, by *instruments*. As the natural tool of unisonous and polyphonic music is the human voice, so the natural tool of harmonic music is the instrument, which now becomes an active factor in musical composition.

CHAPTER VII

INSTRUMENTAL HARMONY

IN the first chapter I stated my intention of giving not a list of names, dates and compositions, but a picture of the influences which have brought about changes in musical form. I find the productive value of historical study not in being informed *that* the Gregorian chant is constructed in one way, the music of Palestrina in another and the music of Bach in still another. Facts of this sort are of course important, but it seems to me more important to ask *why* one sort of music is constructed in one way and another in an entirely different way. According to the theory of development, a highest point must at some time be reached, where the final, the eternal pattern would be found which would then only need to be perpetuated. It is agreed, for example, that the art of Palestrina denotes a culminating point, a perfect balance, that is, of all those forces which are necessary to the creation of a work of art. But if this were actually perfection, it would be folly to attempt to surpass it. Why not continue to compose in Palestrina's manner? Why not continue to compose in the manner of Bach and Handel, Mozart and Beethoven, Brahms

and Wagner? Or why, indeed, did not these men
write the kind of music Palestrina wrote, or why did
not Palestrina compose in the Gregorian style?

We may hardly assume, as seems to be customary
in regard to modern music, that all change is de-
cadence, that music has become impotent and unin-
spired or has in some other way degenerated, simply
because the old forms no longer serve. The true answer is only to be found in understanding that all
form in art is an evidence of our intellectual and
emotional life, and that this life is an incessantly
changing play of creative forces. For this reason there
can be no eternal types of form in art, no eternal
laws, but only the lawfulness of that which is right in
itself. This lawfulness of the right we call beauty, its
achievement we call perfection. The components of
this beauty and this perfection must and will always
change, as all things do. The appearance of new components signifies the awakening of new sensations, a
transformation in thought and feeling, for the creation of something new always necessitates not the
enrichment but the dissolution, the melting over, of
something that has gone before. For this reason also
it is a mistake to compare the value of music in different times, and to ask who was the greater, Beethoven or Mozart, or Bach, or Lassus, or Palestrina,
or the old Netherlanders, or perhaps the unknown
masters of the *Ars Nova* or Gregorian music. There
can be no comparison here, but only recognition of

the varied conditions governing the nature of perception.

All music taken into account so far, from antiquity up to the 16th century, was based upon the original perception of tone as *sung*. The instrument which made air resonant and which gave music its material character was the human voice. But as I pointed out in the beginning, as far back as history takes us instruments were also known as a means of producing tone, so that there has also been instrumental music at all times. Now we find that instrumental music comes to the fore as soon as secular music takes precedence over cult music, as in the later days of antiquity, and again particularly in the Christian *Ars Nova* of the 13th century, before the great period of the Netherlands. But even then the instrument is always combined with the voice, to which it is subservient. At times it overruns the voice, but only as ornamentation. Where the instrument appears independently it is still thought of as the voice and is really used merely as a substitute for it. It is well worth noting that we cannot ascertain definitely whether this old music was intended to be vocal only, or vocal and instrumental. This is a point on which research is of diverse opinions. Perhaps we come nearest the truth if we suppose that it was intended for voices only, but that in practice instruments were added without scruple when there were not enough voices. The instruments were substitutes for the voices and were fashioned accordingly in form and character, aiming at a short, vanishing tone without much carrying power. The lute was the representative instrument, and the purpose of all instruments was to accompany singing.

But now a revolution begins in the effort to make instrumental tone independent in character. To understand what this means we must realize that all instruments, even the simplest, are mechanical. In putting a mechanism, of which he becomes merely the driving force, between himself and tone, man subjects tone to the mechanical conditions of production imposed by the instrument. In time new laws for its construction necessarily result. The voice is a physiological instrument, its tone therefore imposed physiologically determined patterns, and as such we must understand the horizontal time-succession of both the homophonic and the polyphonic phrase. The musical instrument, on the other hand, is a mechanical tool and its tone therefore imposed patterns of a mechanical order, laid down mechanical principles, that is, for the construction of music.

Such a change became possible only with the dominance of mechanical conceptions and the knowledge that natural forces conformed to physical laws. I have just called attention to the revolutionizing effect of the physical view of life. Without this new point of view the awakening of the harmonic sense, the conception of tone as the sum of many vertically grouped tones, would be unthinkable. The harmonic conception in turn developed a preference for instrumental tone, because the composer's imagination was no longer governed to the same degree by the characteristic qualities of the human voice, but was inspired rather by the concord of harmonically ordered tones. The neutral quality of instrumental tone was better suited to harmony than the distinctively individual quality of the voice, which disturbs the pure conception of tone because of its association with sex and language. Instrumental tone was also a better medium for harmonic expression because, unlike the voice, the instrument itself can produce harmonies, while its tones, unconnected with language or sex, are more readily amalgamated into chords than the individual quality of voices.

From this change to harmonic consciousness fundamental alterations in the whole structure of music result. A tone is conceived no longer as a self-contained unit to which the voice gives its characteristic quality, but as a *plurality* of tones belonging to each other. These tones must be arranged with relation to each other in space. The principal tone, the one felt to be the strongest and most dominating, gravitates downwards, and becomes the bass, the *fundamental tone* of the chord. We see here the operation of the force of gravity in acoustics, upon which is built that musical law which we call the law of *tonality*, the relation of all tones to one principal bass tone. This sense of gravity in tonality is entirely foreign to pre-harmonic music, which knows keys or modes only as *successions* of tones. Ambrosian music has four, Gregorian music eight such modes which may be considered in a way as the prototypes of melody or better, of monody, the simplest arrangements of tone used in singing. The later Middle Ages made of these the so-called ecclesiastical modes; they had Greek names—Dorian, Lydian, Phrygian, etc.—and were also monodic types. The succession of tones in the different modes varied according to which tone was chosen as starting point. Thus the mode beginning on C was different from that beginning on D, which again was different from the next.

The awakening of the harmonic sense necessitated the arranging of tones in reference not to their succession in time but to their relative distances from each other in space. Since the effect of gravity in the fundamental tone was always the same, whatever the tone was called, the other tones were also always placed at the same distances above each other. In this way the old modes were changed into the new *scales*. The name "scale" already indicates that we are dealing not with a succession of tones but with an ascending scheme in space, going in single steps from the fundamental tone to the octave. The arrangement of distances between the steps is always the same, whatever the fundamental tone may be, so that these

scales are transposable. Hence there is no longer a different mode on every tone, but there is only *one*
scale, which is called the major scale. By changing one
step, the third, which in this scale is a large or major
third, to a small or minor third, a second scale is
created, the minor scale, in which the succession of
tones differs somewhat from the major but remains
consistent, i. e., transposable, throughout all minor
scales. Harmonic music is built up on the major and
minor modes, as we now call them, which are founded
upon the conception of the bass as the gravitating
fundamental tone.

The lawfulness of harmonic music is easiest to
understand if one takes harmony as the manifestation of the workings of gravity in acoustics. From
this sense of gravity springs the sensation of consonance and dissonance, which is due to the shifting of
equilibrium, the oscillating and stabilizing of sound-
waves. By imagining harmony to be a tapering column of air, we may picture its organic structure.
Since harmony is itself a spatial conception, it follows
that harmonic forms must be spatial forms, based on
activity *in space*. The forces of motion in space we
call dynamics. Dynamics, when manifested in the
activity of overtones, are called *melody;* dynamics,
when manifested in the accented motion of succes-
sive tones, are called *rhythm;* dynamics, when manifested in nuances of rhythmic and melodic movement, loud or soft or medium, are called *gradation;*

and finally, dynamics, when manifested in the variety of tone-quality, are called *color*. Melody, rhythm, gradation, color, are dynamic effects, but dynamics themselves are the force of motion in space, the force which actuates the spatial fabrics of harmony and moulds them into artistic form. To make this as clear as possible, let us realize that air, although invisible, is subject to the same laws of construction as visible matter. Only thus shall we understand that with the strengthening of the physical view of the world, the resonant forms of air, too, were seen to be subject to the play of physical forces, whence sprang the conception of harmony with all its accompanying characteristics—the sense of tonality, the feeling for consonance and dissonance, the scale-system, the artistic concepts of melody, rhythm, gradation and color.

The essential feature in the history of the 16th and 17th centuries is the awakening and gradual establishment of the conception of musical forms constructed upon these physical laws. The actual forms presented to us in notation merely follow as a consequence of this idea. If, when we hear a dissonance, we desire its resolution, or if, when we hear the dominant in the bass, we desire its progression to the tonic, these are tone-sensations in themselves, but they are based upon a sense of gravitation. The science of the harmonic structure and combination of chords might therefore be called a science of gravity acting in the sphere of acoustics. For the second time we observe the connection between music and mathematics, first mentioned in considering the vocal polyphony of the Netherlands. There I spoke of the contrapuntal forms, which seemed so very artificial, as patterns of vocal tone mathematically arranged in time. Now we recognize the instrumental forms, the forms of harmonic music, as patterns of mechanically produced tone mathematically arranged in space. Mathematical laws are effective in both cases; they in no way hamper the imagination, but give it direction. It is only the type of mathematics that changes, being for all music after the 16th century the mathematics of space.

From this standpoint it will be easier to understand what now occurs. The 16th and 17th centuries are a time of invention and perfection in the instrumental field. The instruments already known are improved, they are proportioned in conformity with the acoustic laws that govern the strength and intensity of tone. Gradually the present day forms of the piano, the organ, the violin, the wind instruments, evolve. The materials had been at hand for a long time, but the real stimulus to their development came only with the harmonic idea. Harmony had need of instruments because the single instrument, unlike the human voice, could produce consonant tones. We must think of all these things as happening quite unintentionally and over long stretches of time. The accepted medium is still the chorus of many voices with its polyphonic

forms which gradually become more and more harmonic. Instrumental music meanwhile adopts these
polyphonic forms. They are made use of in organ
music especially, which now attains a growing importance in the church.

With the advance of instrumental music a new
secularisation takes place. We have seen that the last
great vocal compositions were already distinguished
according to their points of origin into Roman,
Venetian, South German, North German, French
and English. In addition to this territorial distinction
in cult music, art-music is now, with the increasing
instrumental trend, penetrated by the secular forms
of dance and song. The urge is felt to give this music,
which gradually takes on features foreign to the old
cult, a new sort of secular form without getting into
the sphere of actual dance and song. From this effort
spring two new types of composition, on the one hand
purely secular and on the other semi-spiritual, the
opera and the *oratorio*. Along with these and the
Christmas and Passion plays which were animated by
the spiritual folk-song and were constantly being
more richly developed, instrumental music grows ever
more vigorous and independent. These are the principal characteristics of music as the 16th century passes
into the 17th.

CHAPTER VIII

THE ITALIANS—OPERA AND ORATORIO —SEVENTEENTH CENTURY

Viewed in historical perspective, the 17th century appears today as a century of manifold experiments, of eager and fanciful invention, and yet as a period of *transition* as well. Itself a range of but middling importance, it connects the great mountain peaks of the 16th and 18th centuries—the time of Palestrina, Lassus, the Gabrielis and the Protestant masters, Senfl and Johannes Eccard, with the time of Bach and Handel. After all that has been said I need scarcely insist that to characterise a period as one of transition implies no estimation of its worth. There is indeed no time that is not a time of transition, and in attempting to compare the 17th century with the 18th, we would be liable to the same error as in judging the music of the old Netherlanders by that of the 16th century, in that we measure what is older and less familiar by the standard of younger and nearer ideas. The political history of the 17th century is marked by the Thirty Years War in Germany, the persecution of the Huguenots in France, and the political and religious feuds in England which led to civil war and

the beheading of the king. It was a time of great
conflict for all musically cultured countries save Italy
and Spain, for the conflicts were of course not confined to religious questions, but involved a rearrange-
ment of the entire economic, political and social structure of these countries.

Italy was spared these quarrels, and so it is easy to
see how Italy once more, for the first time since the
Gregorian days, becomes the centre of European musical activity, the teacher of other nations. Yet these
other countries too produced outstanding personalities in the course of the 17th century. Germany is
represented by *Heinrich Schütz*, who is, next to the
somewhat older Michael Praetorius, the first German
composer of any magnitude, as well as the first to
receive his education in Italy. The leading master in
French music in the 17th century is *Jean-Baptist
Lully*, the creator of French opera and the ballet, who
was, as a matter of fact, of Italian descent. During
the second half of the century there appears in *Henry
Purcell*, who also wrote operas chiefly, the most important and the most gifted composer in the whole
history of English music. These names show that in
spite of the expenditure of strength for other purposes than art, the 17th century is not wanting in
great composers.

If we turn to Italy we find *opera* beginning in Florence and transplanted thence to Rome and Venice,
where church music had continued to flourish. We

find, beside countless composers of more or less merit, two individuals of the highest order: *Claudio Monteverdi* in Venice, who was a leading personality during the first half of the century, and *Alessandro Scarlatti* in Naples, the determining figure in music at the turn of the century. I mention these two names merely to indicate the situation. A great master always presupposes numerous smaller ones, and church music, secular choral music and instrumental music all flourished beside the opera. If opera and its more spiritual companion, the *oratorio,* became the principal types of composition, it was because the entire range of musical activity of the time could be assembled in these two forms: the secular and the spiritual, chorus and solo, voices and instruments.

The effort at synthesis is altogether typical of the men of the Renaissance. Active themselves in as many fields as possible, good fencers as well as good singers, good poets as well as good composers or philosophers, they also sought to unite all artistic expression in one inclusive form. The Greek ideal, which heretofore had been a subject of theoretical study, became the practical pattern of a concrete, positive way of life. Herewith a new kind of artist stepped upon the scene. In the 16th century it was taken for granted that the composer was a singer, as he had always been, just as today we assume that he can play the piano. Perhaps even more emphasis was laid upon his activity as an executant then than nowadays. Palestrina was a singer and singing-master; the position of composer to the papal chapel to which he was later appointed was an innovation especially created for him. Independent composers, as we have them, were unknown, just as there was no music publishing in our sense despite the invention of music printing. The change from vocal to instrumental music affected the composer's position inasmuch as he became an instrumentalist instead of a singer, most frequently an organist. Beside these professional musicians the Renaissance also brought forth a new type of musician, the generally cultured amateur, the *dilettante*.

This musical dilettante of the Renaissance was a thoroughly and professionally educated musician and composer. Belonging to the upper classes of society, he looked at art not as a means of livelihood but as a refinement of life. He approached music as professionally practiced, moreover, with the critical attitude of the well-educated person. The confusion of voices in the contrapuntal polyphonic style must at first have offended this sort of critical sense. The text was found to suffer by such treatment, and altogether this type of music was found to be contrary to the Greek ideal. Thus Greek drama became the standard of comparison but, significantly, the chorus retired into the background in favor of soloistic recitation. In a circle of such dilettantes the first opera came into existence in Florence in 1594. Its most important feature is the prominence of the solo song, which is handled in a declamatory style because of its obvious connection with the language, and supported by a harmonic background of instrumental accompaniment. This new art was first introduced to a small number of friends, later to a larger circle. It inspired imitation, spreading first to Rome and then to Venice, where it found in *Monteverdi,* the capellmeister of St. Mark's, its first great exponent.

If we seek the motive inspiring this movement that emanated from Florence at the end of the 16th century, we shall find it expressed in the idea of a "return to Nature," the same rallying-cry that Rousseau proclaimed 150 years later and which reappears after another 150 years, at the beginning of the 20th century. It is the reaction, in other words, which always comes when some older form of art passes into its hypergrotesque stage. Then the call for simplicity sounds suddenly from some new direction. The simplicity of the Florentines consisted in summarily doing away with polyphony and counterpoint and establishing in both secular and ecclesiastical singing the supremacy and sole leadership of the single, declamatory voice, supported by instrumental harmony. This style of "nuove musiche" is called monody, somewhat inexactly, as monody, strictly speaking, means *un*accompanied solo-singing. Since one of the characteristics of this music lies in the harmonic accompaniment, we should describe it rather as the beginning of the new melodic style, of the type of music in which the melody moves along above a fundamental bass.

Dismissing for a moment all question of "simplicity" and a "return to Nature," two factors of far-reaching influence are to be noticed in this Florentine movement. First, it recognizes the dependence of music on the characteristics of language. In vocal polyphony the word became subservient to the music, but now the reverse is true once more. The relation, however, between music and words is no longer based, as in earlier days, on meter or accent as the dictators of linguistic form. Instead it is the intrinsic emotional content of the word, its *affective quality*, which directs the music.

The second characteristic of the "nuove musiche" is the intentional combination of *vocal* and *instrumental* music. The two are recognized as possessing different tonal qualities and are now combined, in response to a comprehensive artistic idea, into a single higher form, while remaining each within its own particular sphere of activity.

It is easy to see that a movement of this sort might well give an impetus to the harmonic trend of the time but could not develop it with any continuity. In art, where all change is organic, the radical abolition of an old style is never possible. The Florentines, besides, lacked the creative power to carry on what they had begun. *Monteverdi's* great contribution lay in shaping their achievements, which though bold and of genuine worth were still rather tentative, into a vigorous form of art. In his hands the orchestra is more fully treated, with occasional dramatic effects, certain instruments are handled soloistically, the voice is not only declamatory but approaches independence in solo and duet. The future possibilities of the opera lay in this new development of voice and orchestra.

The fact that opera spread with such extraordinary rapidity throughout Italy hangs together with the erection at this time of many theatres, first for private entertainment, then as a matter of business enterprise for the benefit of a larger public. Or, to put it the other way about, the natural vocal talent of the Italians, cultivated through hundreds of years by the church, the reigning princes and the great self-governing cities, combined with their natural dramatic talent, made possible a sudden and surprising abundance of opera houses. When Monteverdi came to Venice in 1613 there was no opera house; the first of the permanent theatres was established in 1637, and they soon numbered twelve.

The same thing happened in other Italian cities, and particularly in Rome. But in the second half of the 17th century it was Naples, which had always been artistically rather unproductive, that took the lead and became the centre of opera, not alone for Italy, but for the whole of Western Europe. The importance of Naples was due to the activity of *Alessandro Scarlatti*. His operatic style differed from that of his senior, Monteverdi, by its greater emphasis on melodious song. Every resource the voice could command was made to serve in unfolding melody, in contrast to Monteverdi's more dignified and serious style which favored the pathos of declamation. Hence the tendency towards the definitely melodic form of the aria, which was a melody, or rather a vocalistic piece, of the song type. Scarlatti also developed the orchestra more fully in conformity with the vivid dramatic effects sought after by the Neapolitan opera, which had entirely abandoned the Greek ideal of the Florentines.

Though opera became more and more the representative type of music in Italy, other forms were not neglected. Monteverdi and Scarlatti were equally active in other types of secular music and in church music. Yet it was inevitable that the dominating characteristics of opera—the melodious treatment of the voice, the contrast between vocal and instrumental effects, the expressiveness of the word increased through music—should have their influence on other forms. Beside opera the *oratorio* flourished. It originated in musical dialogues linked together by a narrator and greatly enlarged by the addition of a chorus. The introduction of the oratorio is generally credited to *Filippo Neri*, the "humorous saint," as he was called by Goethe, who describes his life in the "Italian Journey." It was in Neri's oratory that these entertaining and uplifting spiritual compositions were supposed to have been first performed. They probably grew out of the biblical dramas, the Christmas and Easter stories cultivated all through the Middle Ages, which, according to the circle to which they were addressed, took the form now of folk, now of mystery, now of spiritual plays. Palestrina worked with Neri in his productions of oratorio. This form later developed in Italy, with the use of theatrical apparatus upon occasion, into a kind of opera.

The desire to develop the emotional expressiveness of music is the incentive which determines the forms of opera and oratorio. It is to be noted that this desire for musical *expression* first asserts itself just when the harmonic conception is becoming more and more firmly established. The significance of dynamics in the structure of harmonic forms, of which we spoke in the preceding chapter, is here evident. The expression of emotion is a dynamic quality, and we see in the striving of this new music towards emotional expression the underlying dynamic impulse which gives it form.

Similar events take place with individual differences in the other countries. French opera, which is related in origin to the ballet, because of the nature of the French language inclines less to melodious singing than to rhythmic emphasis and the solemn pathos of recitation. So we find here a type of composition which, in addition to the dance and the small song-form, cultivates the grand, dramatic recitative;

and which, for the rest, does not strive for popularity but is an intentionally *formal* court art. In Germany and Vienna also opera lacked popular appeal and served court purposes exclusively. The best known German composer of the 17th century, *Heinrich Schütz* (born at Köstritz in Saxony) did write an opera on a pastoral play, "Daphne," adapted from the Italian by Martin Opitz. It was performed at Torgau in 1627, at the wedding of a prince, but the text only has been preserved. Otherwise we know little of any German opera, for the princes who could afford the luxury of these establishments manned them with Italians. It was not until the end of the 17th century, in 1678, that a German opera-house was established in *Hamburg,* of which *Reinhard Keiser* later became the chief composer. With him worked Philipp Telemann and the already famous theorist, Johann Mattheson. We remember it today chiefly because Handel worked there for a short time. After some fifty years it went to pieces for lack of stamina. Keiser, its most prolific composer, was one of those half-geniuses, who, in spite of great talent and versatility, lack a really strong creative personality. The German bourgeoisie, moreover, for which it had been intended was not yet ready for a proper operatic art, so the institution finally deteriorated into a burlesue theatre.

Musical interests in Germany, when not in the hands of ruling princes, were still largely ecclesi-

astical, or at least spiritual in nature. Organists of re-
pute functioned in the churches of the great cities,
singing-schools, presided over by cantors, throughout
the country trained their students thoroughly in
church music, while in bourgeois societies and the
collegia musica of the universities, vocal and instrumental music were cultivated. The highest type
of musical celebration, outside the usual liturgy, was
to be found in the Christmas and Passion plays of the
church, while family festivities of a secular nature
—weddings, baptisms, or the taking of office—were
celebrated with popular music. The great figure of
Heinrich Schütz stands alone in the midst of this
vigorous though narrow and bourgeois musical life.
A European in genius and education, Schütz, as
first capellmeister to the Elector in Dresden, was a
person of influence and highly respected, yet he never
succeeded in touching the popular imagination with
his Italianized music, which took mainly the form
of oratorio. But with him the first German composer stepped before the world. The contact with a
responsive and stimulating musical public which he
was denied was now to be realized by the new masters
of the 18th century.

CHAPTER IX

BACH AND HANDEL

ALTHOUGH the reader was warned against considering the 17th century as one merely of experiment and transition, yet this point of view is admittedly pardonable. For the 18th century produces so many composers of the highest rank that the period immediately preceding it grows dim in comparison. This is not only because the new century is nearer to us and consequently easier to understand. It is principally because in the 18th century music enters the realm of experience to which our own time belongs. With it *our own* music begins. We now talk of ourselves, while everything that happened in earlier days seems like some former existence, inwardly related to us yet outwardly odd and unfamiliar.

It has been pointed out that leadership in musical invention wanders from nation to nation, so that the centre of creative intensity keeps shifting. We have seen how, toward the end of the first period of universal catholic church music, it moved to France, thence to the Netherlands and thence again to Italy. Now it turns from Italy northward, and German music becomes the music of the world, absorbing all productive elements, Italian, French, English, into a universal art of German stamp. There were great composers in Italy and France in the 18th century, of course. But all names pale beside those of Bach, Handel, Gluck, Haydn, Mozart, Beethoven. They are the sum and substance of musical culture in the 18th century.

The appearance of this universal German music coincides with the establishing of the *harmonic* idea as the natural basis of all tone conception. Thus we are as much justified in regarding harmonic composition as characteristically German, as in regarding contrapuntal vocal polyphony as characteristic of the Netherlanders although they did not themselves invent it. The course of events in Germany is similar to what took place in the Netherlands. First a *northern* group dominates, the Saxon composers, Bach and Handel, with whom their predecessor Schütz must be included; then the centre of creative intensity moves southward to *Vienna* which becomes the leading musical city during the second half of the century.

Another similarity is also to be noticed. The universal music of the 15th century Netherlands underwent a process of national division in the course of the 16th century, and the same thing now occurred with the universal music of the Germans, the 19th century being, in contrast to the 18th with its unifying influence, once more a time of division into na-

tional cultures. We need not go into the reasons for
the change; at present it suffices to realize that it
took place. If we compare this occurrence with what
happened in earlier times, we see that musical culture
moves in a wave-like motion, now universal, now
national, now back again to a common unity. Only
the spiritual influences differ under which the separa-
tion and the reunion take place. In the Middle Ages
the *church* was the uniting force. In the 18th century
the impulse to reunion is also of a spiritual nature,
but it is *ethical* rather than religious. The spiritual
ideal is now based on the moral consciousness of the
individual and appears in its highest form in the idea
of world citizenship, of the great community of man.

It is not for us to judge here of the individual
composers; we should rather try to understand them
by observing the conditions which governed their
existence. Thus we shall always find that they wrote
the kind of music that corresponded absolutely to the
conditioning circumstances of their time, and that
what we call the forms of their music were the prod-
ucts of these circumstances. An increased emphasis
upon *emotion* lay at the root of the new spiritual
ideal of the 18th century. As I have already pointed
out, emotional expression is a corollary of harmonic
form, for harmony is actuated by dynamic forces
which, in turn, are directly connected with emotion.
If we recognize the fostering of this emotional conception as characteristic of the 18th century, and

that emotion, furthermore, is expressed in music by the whole scope of dynamic activity—melody, rhythm, gradation, color—then we shall have found a point of view from which to observe the composers of the 18th century from Bach to Beethoven, and also a means of detecting the cause of the differences between them which, briefly put, lies in their different treatment of dynamics, in the alterations which took place in their *perception* of dynamic elements. This thought I beg the reader to keep in mind in all that follows.

Harmony is the *simultaneous sounding* of several tones, or better of the constituent parts of the *one* fundamental tone. Hence harmony is a spatial manifestation. Now spatial forms are subject to dynamic laws as laws of motion. All harmonic forms, therefore, are determined by the energy and character of the dynamic forces operative in them. From this point of view we shall understand not only the great uniformity behind all 18th century music but also the events of the 19th century and even of the 20th up to our own time. Only by realising that man from the 18th century on is a *dynamic person,* that composers are now composers of *dynamic music,* that though dynamic types change from Bach up to our own day the fundamental force in them remains the same—only thus does it seem to me that we may understand the transformations that have taken place in musical form.

We have seen that 17th century music sought to re-interpret the old polyphony, in which independent voices were interwoven, from the harmonic point of view, that is, as emanating from the chord. This endeavor, already noticeable in the choral works of the 16th century, led to various forms. The Florentines proceeded most radically by abolishing polyphony altogether. In theory this was all very well, but only in theory, for the voice could scarcely be satisfied for long with the emotional singing of words. Monteverdi made use of intensified expression and rich contrast in the voices and of colorful treatment of the orchestra; the oratorio brought about the development of the chorus; Neapolitan opera gave melody new life by exploiting the charm of the voice in its aria-like compositions. Beside this primarily melodic vocal art, instrumental music, and organ music in particular, developed independently. In this sort of music, melody supported by words was of no use, nor could mere disconnected successions of harmonies be employed. It was necessary to find some way of arranging harmonic successions in forms of their own. This was presented by the scheme of the old polyphonic forms, which were now made into harmonic forms for instrumental use by treating the parts not as independent parallel voices but as segments of a harmonic chord structure.

The process may be described as follows. Static in itself, harmony to take form has need of some dynamic impetus. This it may acquire in two ways. First, where the *emotional quality* of language acts as an incentive, is taken up by the voice and elaborated by typically vocalistic means—ornamentation, florid passages, contrast in the timbre of different voices, etc. This is the foundation of the specifically *melodic* style, the origin of which is to be seen in song only. The dynamic impulse here takes the form of melodic activity which is derived from the bass tone of the harmony, and includes the intermediate tones merely as complementary voices of secondary importance. This form results in the so-called *thorough-bass*, or figured bass system. Even its notation is characteristic. Only two voices are written out, the bass and the melody, the rest being merely indicated by numbers. The bass-line convincingly illustrates the sense of harmonic gravity in the single chord with its fundamental tone at the bottom, while the melody clearly shows how dynamic activity takes shape.

In the second case, the dynamic impulse is not acquired through melodic activity and the supremacy of the upper voice vanishes entirely. It makes use of *all* voices equally, including the inner voices which in thorough-bass only served as filling. Such treatment presupposes greater individuality in the voices, and is arrived at by *transferring* polyphonic forms into the sphere of instrumental harmony. That this is simply a transfer I beg leave to point out. Polyphony and harmony are in themselves irreconcilable. Harmony is always *homophonic,* derived from a single tone; its several voices are not genuinely polyphonic, but are derived from the breaking up of the single line into its chord constituents. They are therefore not independent lines but concomitant phenomena of the harmony. Whatever forms these chord fractions may be shaped into, their fundamentally homophonic character is not affected, for music by nature homophonic can never be polyphonic too. If it makes use of contrapuntal means, however ingeniously applied, they remain but *means,* conventionalized patterns. For the concomitant harmonic voices owe their existence to the one, harmony-giving tone, and so lack the absolute independence which, when several voices are joined together, constitutes the distinguishing feature of true polyphonic music. Polyphony is a republic, harmony a monarchy. If the harmony is derived from the melodic line, the monarchy is absolute; if it makes use of contrapuntal forms, the monarchy is constitutional. But in either case there is only one *king,* the *fundamental* tone from which everything emanates. To unite republic and monarchy in the working out of their ideas is impossible.

I have gone into this explanatory prelude because the early 18th century is commonly supposed to represent the height of instrumental polyphony. The assumption is misleading. Instrumental polyphony cannot possibly exist in music which is harmonic,

since this would be a contradiction in itself. All harmonic music is but ingeniously multiplied homophony, and so it must always be, or it is no longer harmonic. How this multiplication was brought about is
another question, not dependent upon harmonic
premises. The two ways in which it was first achieved
—in the *transfer* of polyphonic forms into a system
of contrapuntal harmonic sequences, and in the
melodic structure derived from the thorough-bass—
we have already mentioned. The chief representatives
of these two types of composition are those two
gigantic figures that stand at the portals of what we
call music in the modern sense—Bach and Handel.

Bach and Handel were of Saxon ancestry. They
came from neighboring towns, Bach from Eisenach,
Handel from Halle, and were born but one month
apart in the same year, Handel in February, Bach in
March, 1685. Like a great double star they appear,
but united only at the moment of their appearance.
For the roads they travelled were as different as their
own natures and as the ways in which, outwardly at
least, their art developed.

All his life long Bach remained within the confines
of his Saxon fatherland. As an artist he enjoyed high
esteem; for the rest, he was a good, solid citizen,
and father of twenty children. Handel was the man
of the world, honored all over Europe, courageous in
enterprise and untiring in energy, lord of his art and
of his life, a man of the heroic baroque type. The

two were alike in one external respect only: they both went blind at the end of their lives. Even after death the contrast between them was carried out. While Bach's grave was forgotten, Handel, who died nine years later, in 1759, was laid to rest in the English pantheon, Westminster Abbey. Yet their very dissimilarity enables us to see them as one in a higher sense, for whatever creative forces this period had to offer met and were united in these two. Therefore we shall discuss them here from the standpoint of the intrinsic similarity of their art and of the conditions which governed it.

Recognition of Bach and Handel, the appreciation of their works, has passed through many phases. They have never been forgotten entirely, and therefore it is wrong to speak of their being rediscovered in the 19th century. Part of their work was indeed neglected by succeeding generations, or rather, each generation picked out the compositions it considered the best and ignored the remainder. So the later 18th century knew Bach mainly as an *instrumental* composer who wrote especially for the organ and the piano. Beethoven studied the "Well-tempered Clavichord" but the great vocal works he scarcely knew. They came to light again in the 19th century, Mendelssohn giving the first performance of "The Passion According to St. Matthew," after nearly a hundred years, in Berlin. After that came another standstill, until research began to direct interest to the other great vocal works, the "Passion According to St. John," the Masses and the "Christmas Oratorio." The cantatas, religious and secular, became known by degrees, the organ and piano music more and more came to be common property, and finally the chamber music, too, particularly that in which solo instruments were used in concertante style, won full appreciation.

With these changing interests, opinions varied as to the composer's personality and the proper interpretation of his compositions. Bach used to be considered a contrapuntist pure and simple, a learned musician who treated music as a sort of mathematics. The romanticists, again, declared that Bach was the arch-romanticist, and should be interpreted with the utmost feeling and expression. Then came another reaction, which claimed that Bach's music was emotional, that its expressiveness was cramped by the formality of his style but lay in the music itself and did not need to be read into its interpretation. To the older view, Bach seemed to be principally a servant of the church, a sort of Protestant Palestrina who also wrote secular music. Later it became apparent that he could not after all be counted simply as a composer of church music, so he was looked upon as a romantic poet. Finally both the poet and the composer of church music were superseded and Bach came to be regarded as the great builder of musical form we consider him today.

The picture posterity has given us of Handel is

GEORGES FREDERIC HANDEL.

Seul Compositeur & Directeur General
de l'Opera de Londres.

Né en Saxe.

not quite so varied but still sufficiently lively. At first he was simply a writer of oratorios. Not much weight was attached to his instrumental music; with all its merits it was considered, in view of Handel's worldly tendencies in other directions, not quite serious and written somewhat for effect. The Italian operas of the first half of his life were looked upon as utterly worthless, youthful errors into which he had been led by the fashion of his time and from which with growing maturity he worked his way up to the oratorio. It is scarcely necessary to point to the radical change of attitude towards Handel in this respect, the reasons for which will be discussed later. The present cult of his operas is a particularly striking example of the instability of opinion at any given time with regard to what is antiquated and what still lives in a great composer's work. Today Handel's operas are in the repertoire of nearly every great opera-house, whereas twenty-five years ago the attempt to perform one of them would merely have drawn a smile from the wiseacres.

We have seen how time has judged of Bach and Handel and the pictures prove the inconstancy of opinion even in regard to those who are indisputably great. We see here not the shortsightedness of posterity—it would be most unjust to say so—but the change in our power of perception which grasps only that which it is fitted to understand. Now let us try to look at Bach and Handel, these two who are so like and yet so different, as *we* today are privileged to see them. Not that this will be the final view. Those who come after us will think otherwise, as those who have gone before thought otherwise. But we must assert against both past and future our right to use our own powers of observation.

CHAPTER X

BACH AND HANDEL, CONTINUED

I HAVE said that the emphasis on emotion was characteristic of the early 18th century, and that it was
expressed in music by the conception of *dynamics* as
the guiding force in the construction of form.
Dynamic patterns were principally of two types: the
melodic, which made use mainly of the voice and is
known as thorough-bass, and the *contrapuntal,*
which made use mainly of instruments and is mis-
takenly called polyphony.

We cannot draw a general comparison between
Bach on the one hand, as the composer of instrumental music in contrapuntal style, and Handel on
the other, as the composer of vocal music in thorough-
bass style, or between Bach, the pious believer, as a
subjective type, and Handel, the worldling, as an
objective type. The distinctions do not hold. For both
were religious but also downright men of the world,
both were introspective as well as objective, both
wrote vocal as well as instrumental music, and both
made use of thorough-bass as well as of contrapuntal
forms. They even chose the same instrument for their

own use, both being famous organists; and indeed
their professional activities were superficially not very
different. Bach, the rigorous cantor of St. Thomas's
church at Leipzig, leading his congregation in the
singing of cantatas on Sundays or the Passions on high
holidays, was not so very unlike Handel, the despotic
director and promoter, conducting his operas and his
oratorios.

But if these comparisons do not hold outwardly,
yet they make it possible to distinguish more clearly
the *essential* characteristics of the two composers. Although Bach and Handel both wrote vocal and instrumental music, figured bass and counterpoint, and
although both were virtuosi as well as teachers of
singing, there did exist one deep-seated difference
between them, out of which all other differences—
even, perhaps, to the dissimilarity of their lives—
arose. This difference seems to me to lie in what I
should call their fundamental *conception of tone.*
Man conceives tone as either vocal or instrumental.
It is immaterial whether the tone itself is actually
vocal or instrumental, the person who conceives tone
vocally will also feel instrumental music as vocal,
and the person who conceives tone instrumentally
will also feel vocal music as instrumental. Today we
all perceive *instrumentally.* If we have come to mis-
understand and misjudge the old polyphonic vocal
music, and to underrate Handel's operas, it is because
our power of apprehending tone has become one-

sided through the prevalence of the instrumental conception.

We cannot take stock of this prejudice intellectually, nor will reflection bring back that which we have lost by it. What we need is a new *perceptive attitude,* and this we are now developing. One of the most striking symptoms of the music of our day is the gradual re-awakening of the vocal conception of tone. We are beginning to break loose from the tyranny of the instrumental conception; we stand at the opposite pole of the movement which ruled the days of Bach and Handel. With this change in mind, let us say that Bach conceived tone *instrumentally* and Handel *vocally.* So that Bach is related to the immediate future in his attitude, while Handel is related to the past. But with the means they used, the opposite is true. The melodic, homophonic figured bass chosen by Handel is more significant for his immediate successors than Bach's contrapuntal style. Thus each is connected in some measure with the past and in some measure with the future, the combination being merely reversed in each case; so that while they are equally great, equally endowed, equally versatile, Bach and Handel are also inseparably linked together.

The first great masters of harmonic music differed then in this respect, that Handel perceived music as vocal tone, Bach as instrumental tone, both starting, however, from the basis of *emotionally* inspired dynamic activity. From this premise everything else follows. I have said that the tone of the voice, naked and resonant, represents man himself. The composer who conceives tone as vocal is driven toward mankind, into the world of human adventures and affairs, for in order to work with this most human material, to stimulate and improve his power of perception, he needs the companionship of people and the world. At the same time, however, he feels the tone of the voice as already so human, that it becomes superfluous for him to consider whether or not it is expressing those emotions which we regard as natural and sincere. So Handel comes to write opera in the Italian style. In describing the polyphonic music of the Netherlands, we saw how mathematical forms were essential to the crystallizing of the warm and flowing tone of the human voice. Something similar, if in a contrary sense, is true of the operatic form to which Handel turned. If we found fault with the abstract mathematical form of the Netherlanders we should here find fault with forms that are purely emotional. Music constructed in part or in whole merely of melodic effects, leaves the requirements of true emotion out of account. Hence the unreality of dramatic figures, the lack of any psychology whatsoever, the incredibility of operatic scenes so apparent to us, yet which we should not criticise if we understood how they came about. The fact is that neither the plot nor the characters count. Only what the voices do is important, the way in which, impelled by dramatic emotion, they are transformed in their melodious progress into beings of a new world of song, where not human destinies are developed but the dramatic possibilities of the voice.

Handel, I have said, was of that heroic baroque type which, overflowing with the sense of its own strength, yearned for more grandiose expression, for a widening out of the smooth simple lines of the Renaissance. From this disposition, which is again the dynamic emotional attitude, Handel's relation to the technical resources and the forms of music developed. At eighteen he came to Hamburg where he made the acquaintance of Keiser, Mattheson and Telemann, and worked at the opera; at twenty-one he reached Italy, learned, during a sojourn of several years, to know Florence, Rome, Naples, and became famous as a composer of operas. Thence his way led, with a short stay in Hanover, to England, where *Italian* opera was just beginning to gain ground after the brief reign of Purcell's English opera. Here Handel worked as composer, artistic director and manager, and in addition wrote chamber music and was active as a virtuoso, all to meet the exigencies of the moment. The failure of this operatic enterprise provided the occasion, but his deep desire to develop the collective possibilities of the voice was undoubtedly the real reason for Handel's turning to the oratorio. At his hands oratorio grows into a sort of heroic *choral opera.* Harmonic music had done away with the independence of the voices, but by this very act had made possible their development as parts of the great chord mass. This, again, is a typically baroque conception. So we need not think of the oratorios to which Handel turned late in his career as the result of a long search for self-expression. They bring to its perfection that musical style in which tone is vocally conceived and carried beyond all melodious solo forms to the sonorous harmony of the chord mass.

As Handel is the exponent of the vocal, Bach is the exponent of the *instrumental* conception of tone. The former must by nature be a man of the world, entering into human relationships, while the latter must by nature be a *solitary* person. He is like an instrument, a piano, an organ; or like a single simple tone which contains the whole gamut of harmonic variety in its own makeup. Finding all inspiration within himself, he needs the world only for material support. Thus Bach's life was spent within the limits of an honorable but traditionally bourgeois career, passing from positions as organist and concert-master in Saxony to that of cantor at the Thomasschule in Leipzig. There was no need of more; it might have harmed rather than helped his work. Though Bach may therefore seem more serious than Handel, this is no indication of their relative worth. The organic nature of the harmonic form of instrumental music

we call counterpoint necessitates a shutting out of the
world. It is to be observed that all the distinctly instrumental composers of more recent times—Haydn,
Beethoven, Bruckner, Brahms, Mahler—were men
of solitary disposition.

For Bach the emotional incentive was not, as with
Handel, the heroic sense of power and the urge for
grander expression characteristic of baroque art. Both
had the exuberance and the consciousness of their own
strength, but they went opposite ways. Bach, the
descendant of a long line of cantors and organists,
is a man of profoundly religious feeling—not to be
confused with mere church-going piety—the emotional expression of which gives artistic form to all
his music. Here again we may find a certain parallel
with the Netherlanders, although not for the same
reason as in Handel's case. While Handel's expansive emotional nature urged him toward vocal expression, Bach's intensity and delicacy of feeling demanded a style of expression which seemed scholastic
and artificial. In interpreting music of this sort, therefore, it is a mistake particularly to stress the emotional element, which being naturally latent in the
music itself, becomes either trivial or coarse if pur-
posely accentuated.

Bach's creative activity included all types of composition then customary except opera and oratorios
such as Handel wrote, in place of which we have the
Passions according to St. Matthew and St. John,

several masses, including the great B minor, the Christmas Oratorio, and five complete sets of cantatas for every Sunday in the year, of which only two hundred, however, have been preserved. To these must be added secular cantatas, orchestral suites, compositions for different solo instruments, chamber music for various combinations, songs and, above all, the organ and piano compositions. This is but a brief summary of Bach's works, the complete edition of 1900 comprising 59 volumes. Bach wrote the greater part of this music for use in church services or for some other need of the day; it was, so to speak, music of an official nature. Even his compositions for the Catholic church, surprising for a Protestant organist, perhaps, were written for practical use at the Catholic court in Dresden. The organ music he wrote for his own needs, the piano and chamber music for private entertainment or to fill occasional orders. School, church, home, social gatherings, town festivities, sometimes an order from outside, offered constant incentives, and we see Bach composing away, completely absorbed in music, producing one great work after another as though he could not help himself, as though it simply had to be.

Bach's apparent exclusiveness was by no means of a narrow sort. He knew and admired the Italian and French music of the day, copied it and arranged it, all in addition to his other activities. He was also interested in the construction of instruments, particularly of the organ, and he even invented an unusual stringed instrument, the viola pomposa. But he was interested most of all in problems of piano tuning. It is a known fact that the tuning of the piano today is not mathematically pure, but adjusted or *tempered*, compromising, that is, between the natural differences in vibration of a tone by fixing a medium pitch. Although C, for example, the fundamental tone of C major, is really not the same as C, the sixth step of E flat major, on a tempered instrument the same C serves throughout all harmonic relations. Thus it became possible to use the whole range of tonalities in one composition and to see in each tone many possibilities of "enharmonic" interchange. Efforts had already been made at some system of compromise. Bach, following the lead of Andreas Werkmeister, who was one of the first to experiment with equal temperament, divided the octave mathematically into twelve equidistant half tones and thus laid the foundations for the modern art of modulation. In this way tempered tones came to be more used in practice than natural tones.

We have spoken of Bach's religious sense as the core of his emotional life. He expresses this feeling in *ecclesiastical* forms only where the church is part of the life of the community, as in those of its activities which deal with the interpretation of the Scripture and the solemnization of holy festivals, the essential value of which lies not in the ritualistic elements involved, but in their human appeal. Thus the structure of Bach's Passions and Cantatas is to be explained. The setting of the Scripture merely gives him, in a way, opportunity for a wide range of emotional expression in words and music. At the same time, he pictures dramatic episodes vividly, and by means of the chorale brings the whole together in a simple and popular fashion. In his treatment of the voice, too, Bach is guided entirely by instrumental feeling. What he writes is not unsingable, but the voice is woven into the contrapuntal network as part of the harmonic texture; its own particular charm is secondary. His choral fugues, like the great Kyrie of the B-minor mass, are well written for the voice but are instrumentally conceived throughout. Their harmonic counterpoint is as far removed from the old vocal polyphony as Handel's solid chord structures. Nor do they depend on the mass effect so often aimed at today in the interpretation of Bach's choral works, Passions and Cantatas. Bach's music is conceived, more than we think, as *chamber music*. It loses nothing of its greatness in being derived from *within* the harmonic organism.

I have sought to picture the true nature of Bach's and Handel's music so far as it is possible to do so in our limited space and without further analysis of their forms. Let me draw attention to one thing more. In both Bach and Handel we are always impressed with the great power of the *basses,* an impression which materially assists the force, the dignity, the thorough sanity of their music, and which is actually due to the fact that the basses are not merely voices but the guiding impulses in this music. The harmony is still conceived as the building up of tones over the foundation of the bass. The voices may move melodically or in contrapuntal phrases, but the bass is always the sustaining force. Gradually, however, a change occurs in this respect. The emotionally inspired dynamic element in the upper voices, which Bach and Handel use for developing the harmonies of the fundamental tone, takes the leadership more and more into its own hands. The unifying power of the basses diminishes, the urge toward emotional expression penetrates and loosens every layer of the harmonic structure. All harmonic music now obeys this irresistible trend. But the two great composers who stand upon the very threshold of this change to which they led the way, remain untouched by it. In Bach and Handel the primal strength of the great harmonic forms dwells side by side with polyphonic complexity. So for us they are truly eternal, undying figures, whose art embraces everything that we call music.

CHAPTER XI

THE SUCCESSORS OF BACH AND HANDEL

BACH died in 1750 and Handel nine years later. Three years before Handel's death and six years after Bach's, in 1756, Mozart was born. Mozart was seven years younger than Goethe, who was born shortly after Bach's death, and three years older than Schiller, who was born in the year of Handel's death. At Mozart's birth, Haydn was twenty-four, and Gluck and Bach's famous second son, Philipp Emanuel, were both thirty-six. Gellert was about the same age as these two, while of the other German poets Klopstock was ten years and Lessing fifteen years younger than the oldest of Bach's children.

Thus the year 1750 marks a sort of pause in the history of German literature and German music in the 18th century. One generation of great composers was active mainly *before* 1750 and the other considerably *after* 1750. In age they are to each other as grandfather and grandson.

Between them stands the middle generation of those who are sons of the one and fathers of the other. It is indeed a middle generation. Equal in its creative genius to neither of the others, it finds its task in the preservation of its heritage and in preparation for what is to come. It is a generation of teachers, of *educators*. It is the trough between two waves, a period of experiment, like the 17th century which stood between the last great masters of vocal polyphony and the first great masters of harmonic instrumental music.

Again I must warn the reader not to underrate a period of transition which is overshadowed by its great neighbors. The musical material it had to work with was perhaps too diversified for the results to be measurable by any absolute standard. Nevertheless this middle generation paved the way for the activities of those who were to come, up to the close of the 19th century. It founded new forms and tried out new methods of construction, and it also established the *external* conditions under which these new forms developed.

Let us first observe these external conditions in order to comprehend more clearly the change which now took place. It was a change in the composer's relation to his environment. A new kind of creative activity set in, going hand in hand with the progress of *social* readjustment which now brought a new economic security to the musical profession. We shall perhaps best achieve an impression of the whole situation if we begin with these *economic* aspects.

The composer of today with a composition to sell

finds a publisher, who buys the work outright or on a royalty basis, prints it and distributes it for sale through the music dealers. There is thus an element of speculation for the modern composer; he writes for an unknown public, scattered all over the world, which simply goes to a dealer when it wants to buy music.

Let us now try to imagine a time when there was no music publisher, no music dealer, no buying public, and no paid composer, when such trafficking in intellectual goods was unknown. Bach would never have thought of a business connection with a publishing house as a source of income, although certain of his works were published. Music had, of course, been printed and engraved for some time. But it was always a complicated and expensive affair, and these editions were really for the amateur only, like our *éditions de luxe*. *Quantity* distribution of printed or engraved music was not thought of. The idea that composition might have commercial value was therefore unknown, and consequently there was no way of protecting the ownership of ideas, as we do with the copyright system. If you liked a composition particularly, you tried to make a copy of it, and in the same way it was permissible for a composer upon occasion to use the ideas or rearrange the works of another composer for his own purposes.

The difference in point of view between this time and ours lies in the fact that in those days music was

written for the sole purpose of immediate performance, its preservation beyond that moment being a
secondary consideration. Today music is printed in
advance of its use. "Occasional" or commissioned
work is an exception, whereas it used to be the rule.
Bach wrote his cantatas for the services of St.
Thomas' Church in Leipzig, and Handel wrote his
operas for special performances and strictly to suit
the voices of the personnel that happened to be available.

The alteration of the whole economic structure of
existence in the course of the 18th century worked
a change in this attitude. As music *publishing* gradually grew, the composer found a new economic foot-
hold and a new relation to the public. His influence
could now extend beyond his immediate environment, he could attract people he did not know,
amateurs near and far, and build up an invisible following. This lessened his dependence on local circumstances and opened a far broader field to his individuality, which now became an important influence in
the establishing of intellectual contacts with other
places and countries.

Not that individual personality had until now been
forcibly circumscribed and might have developed
differently under easier economic conditions. But we
must see the analogy between what happens in intellectual and economic life. The new economic forms
in which musical activity manifested itself gradually

came into being during the 18th century as subjectivism, the idea of individuality, of the freedom of
the individual, gained ground. The growth of music
publishing was of fundamental importance in this
parallel development, for whereas the composer had
formerly to be in the employ of a prince or of a
city and to write his music for practical purposes,
he now saw a new possibility of subsistence. This was
a guarantee of freedom for himself and his work, and
made him dependent solely on the effect of his own
individuality upon an impersonal public.

It was long before this goal was really reached.
Beethoven was probably the first to live mainly on
publisher's fees, which heretofore had only supple-
mented the composer's income; and even in his day,
an official position was still frequently desirable. But
the important point lies in the fact that a new mode
of subsistence was actually developing for the composer. The first step towards this new state of affairs,
the preparation of a new situation in which the
composer's personality was to count, is to be attributed to the generation between Bach and Mozart.

The initiative which brought about this change
was not confined to a single field, of course, for
economic and intellectual conditions are always
closely related. With the progress of the harmonic
conception of music came progress in instrumental
performance, resulting in the rise of a new form of
musical activity—the giving of public *concerts*. There

had been virtuosi before, but they were singers, mostly opera singers, and their performances were largely dependent upon the coöperation of others. Instrumental music brought out the individual more strongly. The instrumental virtuoso—violinist, cembalist, organist —was *independent*. He either needed no support at all in presenting himself or he stood out so far above his assistants that they seemed merely to provide an accompaniment. Thus the so-called *homophonic* forms came to be developed, forms born of the nature of harmonic music, in which a single voice took the lead while the rest merely filled in.

I must remind the reader once more that all harmonic music is homophonic, the lines in which it moves being derived from the chord. The tendency toward the supremacy of one voice grew stronger as the harmonic conception gained ground, and resulted in a turning away from the contrapuntal patterns of Bach and Handel. Now we have seen that these contrapuntal forms, although they still gave the illusion of being so, were not really polyphonic as the old music of independent voices was polyphonic, but were conceived harmonically. Viewed in the light of later developments, they were an obstacle to the independence of the single voice which was finally to subordinate the other voices to its lead.

We now observe that the contrapuntal phrase declines, all secondary voices are compressed into the *chord*, and one leading voice comes to the fore as the dominant melody, about which the musical development centres. Bach and Handel made the polyphonic pattern over into a contrapuntal weaving of harmonic voices. The next generation retains the principle of this harmonic motion, but achieves it by means that are more drastic and intense and yet simpler. The active impulse is now transferred to the upper voice, the melody, which thus becomes the leading motive force, while the dynamics of *gradation* and of *color* which had been of secondary importance, now come to the fore, the first as volume, the second as variety in quality of tone.

The simplest form of dynamic gradation is the contrast between stronger and weaker tones, between *forte* and *piano*. It already appears at the end of the 16th century, and even earlier in the echo effects of vocal music, and is used in the same simple contrast all through the 17th century. This dynamic resource could not be developed very far during the reign of the contrapuntal phrase, for it would have come in conflict with the melodic motion of the voices, to the confusion of both.

Not until melodic activity was concentrated in one principal voice, with the secondary voices accompanying, could dynamic gradation—gradual crescendo and descrescendo, sudden accents, increased and diminished intensity, in short, all the effects, sudden or deliberate, which went to make the new dynamic expression—develop systematically. The accompanying voices meanwhile took on a new significance, losing their melodic independence only to become important factors in carrying out these dynamic effects.

The dynamics of color developed hand in hand with those of gradation. The two are interdependent. A crescendo may be obtained, for example, if one instrument plays first softly and then louder; but the growing crescendo effect will be more marked if several more instruments are gradually added to the first. The abrupt contrast between piano and forte is particularly striking when first one instrument plays alone, and then a whole group suddenly comes in. If the instruments are all alike, all violins for instance, the dynamic effect is purely one of quantitative gradation, but if string and wind instruments are mixed, the effect is one of both quantity and quality, both gradation and color.

Thus a number of new forms of motion are made possible by the consistent development of the harmonic conception of tone: the supremacy of melody, accompanied by the secondary voices and supported by the bass, dynamic color and gradation as means for achieving variety in volume and intensity, gradual or sudden, and in quality of tone. These developments could have meaning only in a time which set store by such dynamic conceptions, which turned more and more toward *subjective* expression in art. Since the contrapuntal patterns were not suitable for this purpose, other forms had to be found, in which melody, gradation and color could freely and fully develop. And to this end the nature of *instrumental* tone was conducive:

String and wind instruments used singly were the logical carriers of melody; used in small or larger groups they could also serve for gradation and color. The simplest forms developed accordingly in music for solo instruments concertante, in chamber and orchestral music. The piano, again, united all the possibilities of other instruments; it could produce melody, gradation, and, if played skilfully, color also. Inasmuch as its old form seemed inadequate to this new task, the mechanical perfection of the piano in these directions now became the principal problem of the instrument makers.

Under these conditions and as a result of such efforts, the *sonata form,* the foundation of all later forms, came into being. Thus it is a form in which the musical action takes place entirely in the development of melody, gradation, and color. It springs from dynamic impulses before which all tendencies to voice leading in the contrapuntal manner vanish.

The sonata begins with the exposition of a single melody, over against which a second melody appears later by way of contrast. Its significance lies in the fact that, with the continuous alteration of each of these melodies in itself and in its contrast with the other, the whole runs its course with cumulative effect. To this end it uses every means for achieving variety—changes in melodic, rhythmic and harmonic structure, in dynamic accentuation and in color. The structure of the sonata movement is essentially gradational, a sort of crescendo, which also tends to the working up of color effects. This intensification is derived from the continual splitting up of the melodic material by the various dynamic means mentioned, which leads eventually, with the further growth of the sonata-form, to the structural principle of *thematic development.*

Thus a form gradually comes into being in which the characteristic order of succession proceeds through a first theme, a second theme, a development, and the recapitulation of both themes, leading to an effective close. Thus it is, at least, where the term sonata designates a single movement. But sonata— which means a piece that is *played* as distinguished from the cantata, which is *sung*—also designates a group of several movements. These, too, are arranged in cumulative dynamic effect and generally lead from a lively opening movement, through a quietly contrasting middle movement, to a rapid last movement. Here again we recognize the fundamental idea of gradually increasing activity.

This idea now leads to a great variety of color possibilities. In solo music it leads to the piano sonata and the sonata for piano with other instruments, in string music to the sonata-like form of the string quartet, and in orchestra music to the orchestral sonata or

symphony. These forms do not spring from any preconceived patterns, but on the contrary develop from
the conditions laid down by the underlying conception of tone as broken up into the overtones of
instrumental harmony. From the very nature of instrumental harmony, then, creative imagination derives the dynamic means—melody, gradation, color
—with which to construct the new musical forms.

CHAPTER XII

HAYDN

WE have seen that the sonata, on which the new forms of instrumental music were built up, emanated from conditions imposed by the harmonic conception of tone, which in turn was an accompanying effect of the increased stressing of emotion characteristic of the time. I have refrained from naming individual composers, for all great changes of this sort take place outside the range of individual influence, and only a single personality here and there may be taken as especially characteristic of some new development. The 17th century and the first half of the 18th had already contributed to the making of the sonata. The violin and piano virtuosi of France and Italy especially had given impetus to various ideas, which Bach and Handel adopted. In addition, a sort of popular instrumental form had grown up in the so-called "suite," a succession of pieces of the dance and song type, the influence of which crept over into the melodic and rhythmic structure of the sonata. The slow movements of sonatas, for instance, are usually based on the song, while the *Rondo,* as its name implies, was originally a round dance in which the prin-

cipal theme keeps appearing in refrain between contrasting sections.

The sonata began as a group of three contrasting
movements, fast—slow—fast, but a fourth movement was later added between the second and the last
in the pure dance form of the minuet. This addition
was made particularly in the string quartet and the
symphony while the piano sonata generally retained
its three-part form. The suite itself, however, a lighter
form of musical entertainment, was not absorbed into
the sonata, but continued to exist independently in
the serenade and the so-called divertimento. It is
evident that, as soon as the bonds of contrapuntal
writing were cast off and the fruitfulness of dynamics
had been recognized, a period of the liveliest inventiveness set in; but it is hardly possible for us today
to review the activity of this period in detail, and
therefore we do not know what share the various
composers had in contributing to the innovations of
the time.

Until a few decades ago, *Carl Philipp Emanuel
Bach,* the second son of the great Johann Sebastian,
was looked upon as the leading exponent of the transition from the contrapuntal to the harmonic style. For
a time Philipp Emanuel was cembalist to Frederick
the Great in Berlin, and he later became director of
church music in Hamburg, for which reason he is
often called the Berlin or Hamburg Bach, to distinguish him from several of his brothers who were also

composers of high standing. Later it was discovered that a productive school of composers had existed in Mannheim under the leadership of *Carl Johann Stamitz,* to which the development of orchestral dynamics and therewith of the symphonic form of the sonata was attributed. It further appeared that in Vienna, where the Hapsburg emperors had always been ardent promoters of music, the new style had also been fostered in characteristic forms.

The question of priority has little interest save for the investigator. It would have been strange if the need for changes in form contingent upon the new conception of music had not found expression in several places at once. The new achievements were the work not so much of certain individual men, as of an entire *generation.* Yet the individual composers should not therefor be underrated. The enormous number of compositions a single one of them producd, shows that the 18th century composers must indeed have been extraordinarily active and must have revelled in all the variety of constant innovation.

The same intellectual activity is reflected in the tendency towards *improvisation.* All composing was really but improvisation. As a reaction from the polyphonic forms which were built after a higher mathematics of tone, the composer now abandoned himself to the inspiration of the moment, let himself be guided in the choice of form by his own emotion. Music not only was the language of the deeper emotions but interpreted momentary impulses as well. The new tone material was still in a fluid state, so to speak, and was handled accordingly, crystallizing but gradually into more settled and rigid forms.

The picture of this transition period is accordingly somewhat hazy and individual composers do not stand out very distinctly. But when the process of crystallization is completed, an individual again appears upon whom all our attention centres. The achievements of his predecessors shine upon him and to posterity he seems the only and all-inclusive representative of his time. This man was *Joseph Haydn*.

Haydn was born in 1732 and died in 1809. So far as age goes, he might have been a younger son of Bach, a brother of Gluck and Phillip Emanuel Bach, or the father of Beethoven. When he was born, Bach had just finished the Matthew Passion, and when he died, Beethoven had already written at least six of his symphonies. His long, full, happy life extended from before the accession of Frederick the Great into the middle of the Napoleonic wars, and was as though divided into two great periods by the appearance of Mozart. Haydn was twenty-four years older than Mozart and outlived him by eighteen years. Thus he was destined to unite all the creative forces of the second half of the eighteenth century, as revealed in the successors of Bach who ploughed for him to sow, in Mozart who reaped the full harvest, and finally

after Mozart's death, when Haydn was old, in the great, inspiring Handel-cult in England.

Haydn had the peculiar good luck of the genius in that he did not come in contact with any of these stimulating influences until he was capable of appreciating their full value and of carrying them further. Born of poor people, near the Austro-Hungarian border, fate brought him in 1759, after all sorts of hardships, to the leadership of a Bohemian nobleman's private orchestra. Two years later, in 1761, when about thirty years of age, he came in the same capacity to Count Esterhazy in Hungary. Here he found a sphere of activity which determined the course of his life. His work consisted of leading the Count's small orchestra, which had been gradually increased to thirty members, and of providing the various compositions for his musical entertainments —orchestra music, chamber music for different combinations, solo music suited to the talent available, church music for special occasions. Haydn's duties as composer were thus manifold, with special emphasis, however, on *instrumental music*. Although he had full freedom in all details he was strictly limited to local resources. His official position was very much like Bach's, save that the setting was provided no longer by school and church, but by the aristocrat's salon, and that the object of his music was not religious uplift but social entertainment.

For nearly thirty years, until 1790, Haydn remained entirely in the service of the Esterhazys and it was not until after the death of Prince Nikolas that he became more independent of his employers. He then enjoyed complete freedom and became a personality in the great world. His fame had already preceded him. From Vienna, where he lived at the Prince's court during the winter, his compositions—symphonies as well as chamber music and piano sonatas—had penetrated all through Germany and even to Paris and London. At the age of sixty, he went to London for the first time to compose and conduct a number of new symphonies. His success was so extraordinary that he stayed another year and then, after returning to Austria for a while, went back to London for the second time in 1794. From this journey he brought back the texts of two oratorios, the "Creation" and the "Seasons," which he now, in his middle sixties, composed, and which were performed at the end of the century. With these and a number of church compositions Haydn concluded his life's work. Celebrated as the patriarch of European music, he spent his last years in Vienna where he died during the French siege in 1809, at the age of seventy-seven.

When we speak of Haydn's works we involuntarily think of the symphonies, the string quartets, and the two great oratorios. This is not strictly correct, for

Haydn also wrote a remarkable amount of church music, vocal music of different kinds, operas and operettas. Yet it is in the composer of quartets, symphonies and oratorios that we see the real Haydn. His importance as creator of a style lies in his sonata compositions. In every field of instrumental music he brought the sonata-form from its improvised and fluid state into concrete shape. He extended its influence into the realm of song by carrying it over into the solo and choral music of the oratorio. From this time on the standard of tone is instrumental, music is exclusively harmonic, and the sonata, the characteristic form in which instrumental harmony finds expression, becomes the basis of all musical form.

Haydn began with the instrumental forms which lent themselves best to the sonata style, starting with the piano, which Philipp Emanuel Bach had made the model instrument for the sonata. He then took the *string quartet* in contrast, as the perfect combination of instruments similar in type but different in register and quality. As chosen by him from among all other possible combinations, the string quartet is really a *single* instrument like the piano, but capable of considerably greater dynamic development. Haydn's treatment of the orchestra, too, with which he lavishly experimented, forces the solo instrument more and more into the background, so that the many instruments now sound like *one*, adding to the dynamic possibilities of the string quartet all the variety of orchestral color.

I have said that certain forms of dynamic activity —the melodic treatment of the upper voice and the development of this melody through gradation in volume and variety of color effects—were prerequisites in the making of the sonata form. These dynamic factors were developed and organized to the point of perfection for practical use in Haydn's works, and it is this perfection which gives his compositions their absolutely classic stamp.

We have come to overlook the purely artistic value of Haydn's works. We point to the humor, the geniality, the serenity of his music as indicative of a harmless, God-fearing nature, unburdened by any modern emotional problems; a point of view which, in regarding Haydn from the standpoint of Beethoven or the later 19th century, fails to take account of a confusion of cause and effect. We have no right to suppose that so great an artist, who had gone through all kinds of hardships and was unhappily married, knew nothing of inner struggles and emotional problems but sauntered through life always smiling. We do not know what Haydn suffered or how far his religion helped him in his conflicts with life. If his music is joyful, it is so certainly not because it reflects a joyful life, but because it is not concerned with interpreting serious personal problems.

Haydn's serenity is no mere genial self-expression. It is what Schiller calls the serenity of art—the serenity which means detachment from life's realities, which is beyond life's littler joys and sorrows. It is the serenity which comes from the free play of artistic skill, of joy in moulding the organic forces of music to the highest perfection in every detail so that they function with the utmost ease and freedom.

Those very characteristics which the 19th century considered childlike and naïve and which inspired the appellation of "Papa Haydn," bring the man particularly close to us today. We begin to understand that this kind of music is not a mere forerunner of the music of great pathos and emotion, but illustrates rather that power of conquering reality which we now once more consider essential in artistic creation.

There are also, nevertheless, many indications in Haydn of the growing *emotional* conception of music. His adagio movements, as well as the introductions to his great symphonies, show many touches of that pathos which was born of the dynamic elements in harmony. Once dynamics had become the determining factor in form they inevitably led to an increased sense of activity and therewith to the intensified expression of passion, impetuosity, ardour and exaltation. Composers of tranquil music are always followed by composers of more and more dynamic music. These tendencies toward the baroque occur sometimes in Haydn's later works, in details of melody-construction and dynamic gradation. In the oratorios particularly we see at just such moments the limitations of Haydn's genius. The parts which are fullest of feeling and which strive for exalted expression, like the great closing choruses, distinctly lack spontaneity. But where Haydn writes naïvely, inspired simply by his art, as in the prelude to the "Creation" or in the magnificent dynamic harmonies of "And There Was Light," he achieves effects which can never be surpassed.

Yet the real Haydn is to be found not in these particular effects but in the character common to all his work. Haydn is the creator of the new homophonic instrumental music, which has completely absorbed the old independent contrapuntal voices and now merely gives form to dynamic activity. It is inspired by the singing voice no longer, but by the mechanical instrument, and thus in its origin goes back to the rhythmic folk-music of the dance. It contains the seeds of its own dynamic development, which is known in music theory as the idea of thematic development. This Haydn carries to exemplary perfection.

Thematic development properly is not a working *with* the theme, but the working of the theme itself, in the free interplay of voices, in the leading of the melodic lines as they are suddenly drawn close or forced apart or as they leap from high registers to low. Development of gradation and color goes with it. Haydn was undoubtedly deeply inspired in later years by the melodic quality of Mozart's music, which —apart from other differences in character between the two composers—was a true *cantabile* conceived in the spirit of the singing voice. This influence enabled Haydn to enrich his instrumental music, which had sprung originally from the dance, with a melodious, lyrical breadth of expression. The influence of the English chorus, too, which he experienced in his travels, together with that of Handel's vocal style and of the broader cast of musical life in London generally, also undoubtedly had an important effect on Haydn's work.

Thus the main musical currents of the 18th century are united in Haydn. He is the first great instrumental composer after Bach. Entirely unlike Bach, Haydn, the master of purely homophonic instrumental music and its resultant sonata form, makes of the string quartet his piano and of the orchestra his organ, thus creating two new means for the presentation of harmonic music. Furthermore, he is the first really great master of oratorio since Handel. Entirely unlike Handel, too, he carries over his purely instrumental conception into vocal music, in both solo and chorus. Contrasting thus utterly with both Bach and Handel, he experiences the miraculous influence of Mozart's genius and is deeply affected by it without his own individuality being disturbed. For Mozart came from another world, to which Haydn could never find the way—the world of the *singing voice*, of *opera*, to which we shall now turn again.

CHAPTER XIII

GLUCK

OUR survey of instrumental music after 1750 and its culmination in Haydn, brings us to the end of the 18th century. But we have neglected another great musical form which flourished in the second half of the 18th century—namely, the *opera*. We followed it up to the moment where Handel turned from Italian opera to the choral form of the oratorio, when the harmonic conception altered the whole structure of music from polyphonic counterpoint to harmonic consonance. In this harmonic amalgamation of the voices lies the peculiar impression of grandeur and yet of simplicity which is characteristic of Handel's music, with its heroic accent on the one hand, its lyric solos on the other.

These two contrasting features of harmonic music —the emotional interpretative quality of melody and the fulness of harmonic consonance—complement each other, making possible a wide range of expression. For this reason Handel could gradually dispense with the dramatic scene as visibly presented in opera, leaving it to the imagination of his listeners in the oratorio. Thus he ceased to write opera although the art itself continued to flourish. Opera now represented one particular form of vocal composition, in which the voice was part of an actual impersonation on the stage, mingling with other voices, expressing whatever emotion the plot required, its charm being enhanced by costume and scenery. This art held so many attractions and offered such inspiring possibilities that its continued existence was assured although a great master had'turned from it.

The secret of its peculiar effectiveness and its lasting strength lay in the double charm of the voice and its visible counterpart represented on the stage. Handel had developed the voice to the complete neglect of the acting. But opera still went on in the old way, and gradually evolved into two main categories based on these two factors. In one, the voice dominated, subordinating all action to its demands. In the other, on the contrary, the development of the action was of greater importance, the voice adapting itself thereunto. The first form was based on singing, on the dexterity of the human throat, all the acting being directed solely towards the display of vocal possibilities. The second form originated not in song but in the dance, in mimetic action and gesturing to music, and treated the voice not as an end in itself but as a means of assisting the action.

There had been no distinction between these two types until the different nations began to cultivate opera, and then the difference became marked. The

Italians, with their instinctively vocal music, and their sonorous language, which is so well adapted to musical expression, strove to develop the virtuosity of the voice. The French, on the other hand, whose music is limited by a language which is musically poor and lays stress on rhetoric accent and on gesture, strove to develop dramatic action. Hence the aria became the nucleus of the Italian form of opera, while the scene became the nucleus of the French form, the former acquiring a vocalistic character, while the latter took on a mimetic character derived from the dance.

These were the two directions in which, under different national influences, it was possible for opera to develop. There was no third national type. Spain, of whose musical history we as yet know little, undoubtedly had a rich musical culture of its own in former centuries, which, however, was scarcely independent enough to be of any importance in the 18th century. England, in the main, was divided between the Italians and Handel, who was largely influenced by them, national opera playing a subordinate rôle and thriving as parody of real opera.

Nor had Germany her own type of opera any more than she had at that time her own literary language or her own theatre. There were German composers of great talent, but if opera interested them they went to Italy. Only in Italy could one learn to sing, and song was the essence of opera. Not only Handel but all German composers went to Italy.

They had to do so, because opera in Germany was a court art and was given entirely in Italian. Berlin, Dresden, Vienna, Stuttgart, Munich, had richly subsidized opera houses, but they served for court entertainment only. The operas were written and composed by Italians, sung by Italian or Italianized singers, conducted by Italians. The German composer had to adapt himself to the Italian pattern and he did so gladly, for he could not have found a more fascinating one.

To these Italianized Germans belonged *Karl Heinrich Graun* in Berlin, *Johann Gottlieb Naumann*, *Johann Adolf Hasse*, the Saxon, one of the most famous composers of the 18th century, and finally *Christoph Willibald Gluck*. Mozart should really be counted as the last of the line, but by the time he appeared Italian opera had already undergone a change. With the constant admixture of foreign elements it had come to be an international art, of importance only as a general form of culture, whereas before it had been essentially national.

Two types of opera developed in Italy: *opera seria* and *opera buffa*, serious and comic opera. They did not originate in the spoken drama any more than opera in general did; they are not tragedy or comedy set to music. They developed from the possibilities of vocal effect inherent in the Italian language. A form like the opera buffa with all its charm and finesse—with the graceful play of its melody, the *parlando* of its

Gluck

recitatives, the fluent clarity of its ensembles—could only have sprung from the formulation in music of the effervescent, tuneful, sonorous qualities of such a tongue.

Opera buffa is therefore the most characteristic of all Italian operatic forms, and the most difficult of imitation. Neither French nor German comic opera can compare with it. They both use dialogue extensively and the music is only episodic, while opera buffa is music from first to last, uninterrupted, the product of a language saturated with music. Opera buffa thus remains the exclusive possession of the real Italians, while opera seria was largely taken over by the Italianized Germans. Opera seria was based on the art of singing, on the melodious development of the voice in varied emotional expression—repose, passion, anger, love. All of which could be learned, being a matter less of individual national temperament than of cultivating the voice.

How far it was customary to cultivate the voice, and at the same time to what extent it had already ceased to be considered as a human organ and treated instead as an instrument of song, is shown by the fact that castration was practiced at this time. The emasculated voice is but an artificial instrument. At its best it seems to combine the charm of a woman's voice with the volume and power of a man's; but in reality it is neither, most unreal and unnatural. The object of this practice was to develop vocal skill, to foster the voice as an instrument only, apart from any human individuality, and to this end all the resources of stagecraft and of music were employed in giving background and harmonic support to the melody.

Such were the conditions under which Gluck, too, began to work. The composer was the servant of the singer. He had to cut his cloth to fit his model, as the tailor by skilful cutting brings out the good points and hides the defects of the figure he is clothing. We should think of the demands made upon him not as indicative of an inartistic attitude, but as being imposed by a vocal art we are no longer familiar with. It is evident, too, that the harmonic conception of music had now arrived at the stage where the whole sense of dynamic activity was concentrated in the melody.

Now as the nature of harmonic form made itself felt more distinctly, the partiality for pure melody as expressed in the beauty of the voice diminished. The dynamic forces of emotion began to influence form more and more. The singer's importance as a model came to be questioned, the voice lost its despotic power and had to be content with whatever place the composer assigned to it in the whole structure of his composition.

The autocratic rule of purely vocal music thus gradually gives way to a harmonic form expressive of dramatic emotion, richer in modulation, with well-developed effects of gradation and color. It is the composer who creates it, instead of the singer who is exploited by it, who now becomes the most important factor in opera. Upon this change is based Gluck's so-called *reform*. It is a form accomplished not through revolution but through the organic development of harmonic forms. The supremacy of the voice disappears. Melody is no longer an end in itself; it becomes part of the harmonic whole, but—and this must not be forgotten—it is still carried by the voice, and so still gives direction to the whole.

In this way a rapprochement is effected between the vocal opera which had its origin in Italy and the dramatic opera of the French. After Lully, French opera had been further developed by *Jean Philippe Rameau*. The possibilities of greater activity in modulation combined with the rhythmic stimulus of the French language made it possible to relate music more closely with gesture and action. To this day, the French people consider Rameau, who was as much a philosopher and a theorist as a composer, as the typical representative of French opera because of the way he balanced the voice and the orchestra, interwove song and gesture. As an artist he was reflective and critical rather than spontaneous, and accordingly his declamation combines singing and recitative, his melody is stamped with the rhythm of the language, his musical dynamics accord exactly with his dramatic effects, all showing that combination of cool logic with mastery of technique which the intellectually keen Frenchman considers typically French.

For this reason, in spite of his triumphs in Paris, the French always regarded Gluck, as they later did Rossini, Meyerbeer and Wagner, as an intruder. The national reaction of the 19th century kept returning to Rameau. Yet we may understand why Gluck's great European successes began in Paris. He had abolished the supremacy of the virtuoso singer, using instead harmonically developed forms, thus leaving the realm of pure Italian opera and approaching that of French opera, with its scenery, dances, wealth of dramatic elements and rhetorical pathos. In bringing to French opera all the beauty of the melodic Italian style, he gave it an impetus which it could never have found in itself.

For song as such is alien to the French language and so also to the French temperament. The purely melodic line of the voice lies outside the French conception of tone, the musical element of the language consisting in the vitality of its rhythm. For this reason Rousseau found himself obliged to deny that his countrymen were capable of great dramatic music, urging them to adhere to the smaller light opera, interwoven with *chansons*. For the same reason the opera buffa of the Italians found enthusiastic reception in Paris, seeming more natural to the Latin temperament than their own rhetorical declamation. Lyric tragedy became symbolic of the *ancien régime,* while opera buffa stood for modern art.

When Gluck first came to Paris, therefore, as he did in 1774 at the age of sixty, to rehearse his "Iphigenia in Aulis," he found not a few obstacles in his path. The followers of Italian opera turned violently against him, calling his music cold and scholarly, and only the admirers of the old French operas of Lully and Rameau stood by him. As in all affairs involving the theatre, much controversy was stirred up, pamphlets were written pro and con, theories were advanced and overthrown. After his first great success Gluck undertook to rewrite for the Parisian public several of his earlier operas, which had been composed in the Italian style, by making considerable changes, shortening here, extending there. Thus "Orpheus," written twelve years before, in 1762, and "Alceste" written in 1767, came to Paris. Then in 1777, three years after "Iphigenia in Aulis," "Armida" was performed there, and finally in 1779, the finest of all his works, "Iphigenia in Tauris." Herewith Gluck's world-wide victory was confirmed, nor could the weakness of his last work, "Echo and Narcissus," detract from it.

Gluck, a forester's son, born in 1714 in a little town on the border of Franconia and Bohemia, had always looked upon Paris, as he had looked upon Italian cities and London, merely as a place where his operas might be performed. From 1750 until his death in 1787 he made his home in Vienna, where he conducted the court opera from time to time and enjoyed the highest esteem of the imperial family and the aristocracy.

It is difficult to speak of Gluck, inasmuch as we know only part of his work and that the later part. For a long time this was true of Handel also, and it seems not unlikely that in view of the newly awakened interest in the old vocal opera, we may soon see a revival of Gluck's earlier operas similar to the present Handel revival. We shall then have to overcome, as we have done in Handel's case, a prejudice history has given us concerning Gluck. While Handel had always been looked upon as a composer of oratorios only, the 19th century has come more and more to regard Gluck as the Wagnerian type of "reformer," the representative of a realistic musical drama.

This is a misrepresentation, to correct which we must make clear what it really was that Gluck fought against. He objected to writing melody to suit the accomplishments of some particular singer, melody, that is, representing purely vocalistic skill. The melody of true song was to him the highest and finest type of music, as we know beyond a doubt when we hear his operas.

Gluck merely brought about a change in the point of view from which melody was written. He regarded melody no longer as a means of displaying a beautiful voice but as part of the music itself. But music to him, in turn, meant purely harmonic music, expressing the human emotion going on in the dramatic action. He liked his action simple, clear, grand, concrete. He therefore chose heroic plots with little external incident but plenty of strong emotion—Orpheus bringing back his lost love from the nether world; Alceste, who dies for her lover; Iphigenia, about to be sacrificed for the sake of her people; the other Iphigenia, who saves her brother from a sacrificial death—themes which centre about one simple but profound idea from which they draw their dynamic power, the triumph of love over death.

Here the attempt to express an idea, a *personal* attitude, is clearly apparent. It penetrates the whole structure of music, lifting it from the mere play of tonal effects to the level of true emotion. The fulfillment is as yet remote: the idea is feeling its way towards expression but is not actually realized. Here Gluck again resembles Handel, as he does in his vital and energetic personality and in his love of the heroic. Musical forms now become increasingly expressive of personality; composition becomes more and more subjective both in its process and in its aims. The great composers, the leaders, themselves grow to be men of gigantic stature. The dynamic revolutionary spirit of the closing 18th century also appears in music, on which the composer now sets the stamp of his own personality.

CHAPTER XIV

MOZART

WE have seen in our survey that the music of the 18th century was pre-eminently German, and that the center of musical intensity in Germany varied, moving from north to south. Bach and Handel were Saxons, Gluck a Franconian, Haydn an Austrian, Mozart a Salzburger of South German descent, Beethoven a Rhinelander. Beginning with Gluck, they all migrated to Vienna, which now became the musical metropolis of the world. The music which emanated from Vienna was a cosmopolitan music. The idea of the freedom of the individual and of man's natural rights, which had gradually become the nucleus of thought and conduct, could only manifest itself in the desire to picture an ideal humanity; for when man becomes aware of himself as a representative of mankind and declares himself accordingly, his highest ideal must inevitably become the brotherhood of all men. The believer seeks a congregation of the faithful, the patriot seeks a national community, the individual seeks the brotherhood of man.

All the great Germans of the 18th century were idealists of this type, not alone the musicians but the

W. A. Mozart.

poets and philosophers also. If they were acutely conscious of their individuality and eager to make the most of it, the higher justification for their attitude lay in the current idea of service to mankind. We may share or reject this idea, we may think that the ideal world these people created in their works was utopian or we may consider it the only worthy form of existence. But in any case we can best understand the creative activity of this generation by realizing the assumptions on which it rested. In expressing both individuality and the love of humanity, two conceptions which seem to contradict but really complement each other, it rose to the expression of an idea which in its breadth made possible the development of an art at once universal and intensely personal. This art mingled the sacred with the secular, absorbed all differences of faith, of race, of nationality. And in its midst the artist stood alone and free, the high-priest of humanity, the prophet of wisdom and beauty, the messenger of eternal peace.

Such a man was Beethoven, and such a man above all was *Mozart*. I have pointed out that with Gluck and Haydn music had reached a stage in which the composer's desire to express his own ethical ideas replaced the impersonal spirit of art. Whether this change was brought about by individual composers or lay in the spirit of the time, whether harmony could not have developed otherwise, or whether the trend toward harmonic instrumental composition merely reflected the general temper of the period, a Mozart could not have come into being save under such conditions. Mozart's style used to be called rococo, meaning that it was merely dainty, graceful and ornamental. He was celebrated as a composer of beautiful and elegant music, balanced, polished, *classical,* music so transparent and serene that it floated beyond all earthly things, remote from Faustian problems and conflicts, music woven only of sunlight and the fragrance of blossoms and a quiet, happy laughter.

The formal perfection of Mozart's art is such as to justify much of this interpretation, especially if viewed from the distance of a later time. But Mozart's contemporaries thought otherwise of him than we do. They found him for the most part difficult to understand, too serious, too complex and artificial. Without going too deeply into these opinions, we realize at once that the notion of Mozart as the god of rococo music does not agree with the personality or the artistic nature of the man. Mozart is a *revolutionary* spirit, the great apostle in art of a free humanity. He is the first to stake his whole life in the struggle for the preservation of his freedom, and he is the first composer whose art *directly* reflects his personality and his ideas.

Mozart is not of the defiant, Promethean type of Beethoven. The two differ in their individual expression but not in their essential nature. In Beethoven's music the conflict itself is expressed, the underlying dynamic urge is vividly apparent. With Mozart the conflict takes place for the most part outside his music, precedes the act of creation, but it is the assumption upon which his art rests. The fact of mastery achieved gives us the impression of perfection. Let us grant the perfection and call it divinely inspired if we will, but we must not forget that it has come none the less from that invisible personal battle, the struggle of the individual with himself, which Beethoven so drastically depicts.

In calling Mozart a revolutionary, I refer less to the political revolution than to the revolution in thought and point of view which was now preparing and which was characterised by Rousseau's slogan, *Back to Nature*. This idea of a return to nature, meaning a return to a more natural human standard, governs Mozart's whole life and work. All his problems are conflicts between nature and unnatural convention, and nature is his criterion in solving them.

Mozart was brought up in strict servitude to a pious court, in which he and his father held official posts, but he severed this connection when a natural desire for freedom forced him to do so. He grew up with the highest respect for his father's authority, but impelled by his own nature he defied that authority and married against his father's will. Ambition for office and titles, all the sycophancy then still common in the musical profession, were alien and hateful to him. All he wanted was to earn money enough so that his family might live and he might compose. He was a religious man, but a skeptic regarding the doctrines of the church. The whole trend of the period of "the Enlightenment," which went with the movement back to nature, had its influence upon him too. He became a free-mason because free-masonry realized the ideals of human brotherhood, of a peaceful, happy future for mankind. What we know of him through his letters, his conversations and his actions, shows a man untrammeled and unwarped by circumstance, natural in thought and speech, who knows no half-heartedness, no falseness, no affectation, a man who is true to the last fibre of his being, in whom, we may say, Nature and Man are identical.

Herein lies the unique and inimitable quality of the man and of his music. It would of course be foolish to ask who is the greatest genius, Bach or Handel or Mozart or Beethoven? But if we would point out the essential characteristic of Mozart, wherein he differed from the others, we cannot do better than indicate this absolutely natural quality of his personality and of his art. The special characteristics of great men, that which we call their genius, are various and always new, but there has never been a better example than Mozart of the truth expressed in Goethe's maxim that "Art and Nature are but one."

Thus it is that in the entire known history of music, we find no comparable example of genius manifesting itself so *early* with such elementary force. There have been musical prodigies before and since, to be sure; but Mozart's productivity surpasses that of all others in facility and worth. We know that he had an excellent teacher in his father, who endeavored above all to give his son a broad view of the world and of existing styles of composition. So Mozart went as a child from the little town of Salzburg to Vienna, Munich, Mannheim, to Italy, to Paris, to London. His father took him wherever music flourished and he responded keenly to it all. These travels must also have contributed to the development of his innate conception of humanity as something over and above nationality, by teaching him to recognize a common spirit reconciling all human differences. If in foreign countries he was doubly glad to feel himself a German, and liked to emphasize the fact, it was because he was conscious, not of being different, but of making the culture of his own country, which was not yet recognized, known to others.

We also know that the infant prodigy's success was followed by a period of disappointments. It is not fair to attribute these disappointments altogether to the indifference of the world. They lay for the most part in Mozart himself. He was not a man for this world, he could not adapt himself to it as far as would have been necessary to the pursuit of a brilliant career. The sensational attraction he exercised as a prodigy died out and, unconcerned with custom and contemporary opinion, the grown man followed his own path, a path more difficult than that of other musicians. Thus he soon joined the ranks of those composers and virtuosi who were accorded esteem rather than enthusiasm. The outward circumstances of his life rapidly became worse and with advancing years the shadows deepened. Mozart was a free man, but the world took little heed of his freedom. He was a much admired pianist, but there were others the public preferred. He was a respected composer but there were others more popular, and at times his operas— notably "The Marriage of Figaro" in Vienna—were only performed after many struggles against intrigues of every sort.

Mozart could not have been Mozart had he been so constituted as to fare better in life. He managed his household affairs poorly. When he had money he spent it, and he always had occasion to spend, for he loved life. He was not dissolute, as has sometimes been said, but straight-laced hypocrisy of any kind was foreign to him. He was tenderly devoted to his wife, but that did not prevent him from caring for other women. He was no gourmand, but he could honor the attractions of a good table. In all respects he was a man who knew well what was great and good without disdaining little things, a man who carried his standard of behavior in himself. Therefore, he was bound to give offense wherever this right to moral self-determination was not recognized.

This was the human spirit which underlay his art.

Mozart was active in every field of musical composition. He wrote instrumental music of all kinds, concert music for the piano and for other instruments, chamber music for the most varied combinations, orchestral serenades, divertimenti, symphonies. He wrote vocal music, secular and religious, masses and other liturgical compositions, oratorios, concert arias and duets, songs, pieces for social entertainment. And all in the short span of thirty-five years. Although most of his music is still very much alive, at the mention of Mozart's name we instinctively think first of his operas. This is not only because of the popularity of opera as a form of music, but because Mozart's operas undoubtedly occupy the first place among all his works. Not that they are superior to his other compositions as works of art, but because Mozart's inmost nature, his humanity, is most apparent in his operas.

Mozart began by composing Italian operas. He came to Italy as a boy and, according to the prevalent custom, was commissioned to compose operas for a certain theatre with a given personnel during its season. Italian opera laid the foundation of his operatic style throughout. Only two of the operas still played today have German texts, "The Abduction from the Seraglio," which he wrote when he was twenty-five, and "The Magic Flute," which was performed for the first time in September 1791, a few months before his death. Both trace their origin back to the German song-play which consists of a succession of songs and other vocal pieces interspersed with dialogue. Italian opera had no dialogue, only arias, ensembles and recitative. There were two kinds of recitative, the so-called accompanied recitative, in which important, dramatic recitation was accompanied by the orchestra, and the *secco*, or dry recitative, in which the words were rapidly enunciated, half-spoken, half-sung, without melodic expression, accompanied by the cembalo alone. Mozart did not write any French operas, as no occasion offered and the heroic pathos of the type was not natural to him. Except for his very early Italian operas, he wrote only one work in the *seria* style, "Idomeneo," which he composed for Munich in 1781.

Here already we see how Mozart differed from Gluck, with whom, indeed, he had conspicuously little in common. They were dissimilar not only in nature, but even more markedly in their approach to music. Although Gluck had replaced vocalistic melody by emotionally expressive melody, he nevertheless remained the objective composer, casting a light, as it were, from without inwards. All he did and all he wanted to do was to depict the action in the music. Mozart worked not from without inwards, but from within outwards; he pictured not man but the soul of man. His melody is not descriptive, it is the outpouring of human emotion. But Mozart did not aim at dramatic plausibility as did the later romantic school of opera. In this respect opera will always be inadequate. Man appears unnatural enough in singing, and if in addition he performs artificial arias or joins others in vocal ensembles, it is a foregone conclusion that the result will be unrealistic. Real human interest is never to be found in some logical carrying out of plot or character, but only in the way natural emotions are transposed into musical action, into melody that is impregnated with harmony. For this reason Mozart declared that in the opera "poetry should be the obedient daughter of music."

For this shaping of melody out of the very nature of human feeling Mozart needed the stimulus of texts containing some realistic human interest. Thus we encounter the first really human operatic types in his works. They lack the pathos and rhetoric of Gluck; they are unceremonious, everyday characters, as in "Figaro" or "Cosi fan Tutte," or in most of "Don Juan" and the "Magic Flute." Then again they are figures meant to emphasize the extraordinary, like the Stone Guest, or Sarastro, or the Queen of the Night; but even this very quality of the unusual is of a purely human sort. Mozart tells the tale of his opera in melodious song. His melody is Italian in form but imbued with a German warmth of feeling, reflecting the soul of the story in its natural simplicity. In discussing the music of the Netherlands, I said that the singing voice represented man in all his nakedness. It is this very nature of man which Mozart gives us in his melody, achieving the expression of it not through any psychological approach, but through a singular power of divination.

This always melodious quality is the foundation of Mozart's instrumental music also, and it gives us the key to his relation to Haydn. From a historical point of view concerned purely with the development of the elements of form, Haydn is more important than Mozart, who could, in this sense, be more easily left out of the story of instrumental music. The whole technical development of instrumental harmony, which was of such importance to Haydn in the construction of the sonata, was of secondary interest to Mozart. While Haydn achieved an always more distinctly thematic style of melody, which was finally reduced to a most flexible handling of motives, Mozart's instinct for song, on the other hand, drove him towards an ever richer breadth of melodic phrase. Herewith he achieved an inner vitality, diversity and individuality of melodic expression which could only have been inspired by the quality of the human voice. While melody lost the charm of this human quality in the transfer from vocal to instrumental music, it was, on the other hand, no longer confined to the leading voice alone, but penetrated deep into the whole harmonic structure, giving it a wealth of *modulation* heretofore unguessed, even by Haydn. It is in the introduction of vocal melody into instrumental music and in the development of harmony by means of modulation, that the significance of Mozart's instrumental composition lies; it is this which explains his own leaning toward instrumental music, and it is this also which distinguishes him from Haydn.

After his death the world's neutral attitude toward Mozart changed to an admiration such as has scarcely been accorded to any other composer. Easy as this may be to understand, we must beware, especially in Mozart's case, of mistaking the true causes of his universal influence. They are not to be found in the formalistic qualities of his art, its grace, balance, clarity, in what we call the "beauty" of his music. I have defined beauty as what is right and true in itself, though the elements which go to make it up may vary. The particular beauty of Mozart's music lies in its picturing of a supremely free and natural human existence, unencumbered by convention and prejudice, idealizing Nature and Man, who is at once the creature and the master of Nature.

CHAPTER XV

BEETHOVEN

MOZART and Beethoven have sometimes been compared to Raphael and Michelangelo, respectively, by way of illustrating the difference between balanced perfection and titanic greatness. Parallels have also been drawn between Mozart and Goethe on the one hand and Beethoven and Schiller on the other, by way of contrasting the naïvely natural with the emotional and reflective genius. Comparisons of this sort may be stimulating and enlightening if not carried too far, but it seems to me that those just mentioned denote on the whole superficial rather than intrinsic similarities. There is to my mind only one figure in the entire history of art to be compared with Beethoven, and that is Rembrandt. Both hold us spellbound by the same *force of expression*, manifest in the same power and depth of emotion, the same exalted spirit. Both, notwithstanding all the dissimilarity of the materials with which they work, use the same medium of expression, *dynamics*—Rembrandt the dynamics of light, Beethoven the dynamics of tone. And both employ the same matchless economy of artistic resources, possess the creator's absolute control over emotional forces, the sovereign integrity of the artist who never loses sight of his object, but who, even in the moment of highest ecstasy, is still clearly master of his art. I am not comparing Beethoven and Rembrandt for the sake of adding another partially apt parallel to those already mentioned; but if parallels are to be drawn at all this seems to me the only one which touches the essentials.

With Beethoven the musical classicism of the 18th century enters upon its baroque stage. If by "classicism" we mean the perfect balancing of all elements in a work of art, the control of self-expression through principles of form, the general typified by the particular, "baroque" in turn stands for irregularity of line, the driving of forces from within, the stressing of the contrast between tension and release. Herewith emphasis begins to be placed on what we call *expression*. The sweeping lines, the exuberant, spasmodic, constantly changing forms of the baroque style in every art may be summed up as the urge toward expression for its own sake. In music this style is called *espressivo*. With it personality steps upon the scene in all its individual distinctiveness. It is no longer man as the representative of human kind, but the individual with all his own particular peculiarities, who becomes the subject of observation and treatment both in the sciences and in the arts. Beethoven is an example of this individual distinctiveness. Dependent upon himself alone, growing only from within, he interprets life through his own vision and his own feeling. He does not come to be like this through any accident of fate. He *is* so from the moment he steps into the world, and all that he experiences can only serve to affirm and deepen his innate consciousness of self.

Beethoven was born in 1770 in Bonn, where his father was a singer in the electoral chapel. Here, as a boy of about twenty, he watched the drama of the French Revolution, which occurred during the last years of Mozart's life, and experienced its after effects at close quarters. The idea of freedom and the rights of the individual, which to Mozart was a matter of personal opinion and point of view, became for Beethoven the actual pivot of world-rending political events which took place in his adolescent period, when man is most receptive and character receives its determining stamp. They decided the tenor of his life so far as any outside influence came into question. Beethoven, who was not a prodigy like Mozart although his gifts were early recognized and won him patronage, went to Vienna at this time. He took lessons from Haydn at first and later, when Haydn's teaching seemed to him not careful enough, from other excellent though less famous musicians. The extraordinary power and technical brilliance of his piano-playing soon attracted attention, and he became especially marked for his skill in improvising. Though he was fundamentally different from Mozart by nature, in-

considerate, defiant, proud, he soon found access to aristocratic circles to which he adapted himself without in the least subordinating his individuality.

He was spared material worries. His compositions were sought after by public and publishers alike. His relations with the latter, indeed, had now reached the point where the sale of his compositions brought in a fair income. Beethoven's life in Vienna might thus have followed an untroubled course had not deafness set in as he neared the age of thirty. It grew steadily worse and led at times to fits of despair, like that reflected in the Heiligenstadt will of 1802. Beethoven was by nature of a cheerful, strong, exuberant disposition, a child of the 18th century, neither melancholy nor pessimistic. Nor did he ever become so, although his increasing deafness rendered social intercourse difficult and made him irritable and suspicious in his personal relations, while he had much trouble to bear during the last decade of his life from his nephew Carl, whom he had adopted as a son. Financial worries such as Mozart had suffered, Beethoven never experienced. When in 1809 he was invited to Cassel as capellmeister to Jerome Bonaparte, the nominal King of Westphalia, three Viennese aristocrats joined in guaranteeing him an annuity so that he might remain in Vienna. In subsequent years the annuity diminished through depreciation of the currency, and Beethoven was forced to claim payment of the full amount due him by process of law. Incidents like this, however disturbing in themselves, did not seriously endanger his economic welfare. Thus Beethoven spent his whole life in Vienna and its environs, after plans for longer trips to Italy and particularly to England had again and again come to naught on account of his deafness.

His prestige in Vienna, Germany and England was unchallenged: nobody, especially during the second half of his life, would have dared to doubt Beethoven's priority among living composers. His works formed the centre of musical festivities during the congress of Vienna, and the story that his later compositions met with little sympathy is a myth. The performance of a new work by Beethoven, whether a symphony or a quartet, was an event of extraordinary import. If the receipts from the first performance of the Ninth Symphony fell below Beethoven's expectations, it was because of circumstances which impaired neither his popular nor his artistic success. He was the great master, to be met only with reverence. No stranger of prominence failed to visit Beethoven, provided Beethoven would receive him. He enjoyed relations of friendship with intellectual leaders of his time—with Goethe, particularly, whose genius he deeply revered, with certain of the romantic poets, Bettina von Arnim, Tiedge, Elise von der Recke, and with the Austrian poets, Collin and Grillparzer. Beethoven always found inspiration in literature and philosophy. In Homer, Shakespeare, Ossian, and in the poetry of his contemporaries also, he took a lively interest. He once wrote in a letter: "No discussion is apt to be too deep for me. Without pretending to be really learned I have always endeavored, from my childhood, to grasp the thoughts of the better and wiser men of every age. Shame to the artist who does not feel obliged to go at least thus far."

These words picture the real Beethoven and bear witness to the conception he cherished of the nature of his art. He lived to himself, away from the world, from which he was all the more separated by his deafness, although he never became misanthropic or cynical. He was a great man, the unique artist, filled with the consciousness of his own greatness, but none the less able to enjoy innocent fun and cheerful pleasures. A kind-hearted, affectionate man in the truest sense, he was like Mozart, like Haydn, like Schiller, like Goethe, like Kant, a citizen of the world, reaching out beyond all barriers of religion, nationality and race. He is the youngest and the last of those great men whose ideas encompassed the universe and whose love embraced all mankind.

Beethoven died soon after the completion of his fifty-sixth year, in March 1827, in Vienna. He was buried with the honors becoming a prince, unlike Mozart, whose funeral nobody attended and who was laid in a pauper's grave. Beethoven seems to have produced considerably less than Mozart though he lived more than twenty years longer. He wrote only one opera, only nine symphonies, sixteen string quartets, thirty-two piano sonatas, chamber music for piano with various instruments and for winds, two masses, one oratorio, concertos, songs and smaller compositions. The number of his works is less than that of any of his predecessors, but each composition is of incomparably greater importance. We have seen how up to Haydn's day instrumental forms had been in a fluid state, as it were, and how they were only crystallized out by Haydn. This crystallizing process continues with Beethoven and music at his hands grows always more and more condensed. It steadily gains in specific gravity, as it were, grows heavier, more closely compressed, capable of more vigorous utterance. It becomes massive, like matter grown rigid. And so it strives towards monumental forms, and turns the process of construction into an intensive struggle of the artist with his material.

The analogy may serve to picture more clearly this process of condensation in Beethoven's writing. When we speak of tone-material becoming rigid it is only in the sense of compressed *intensity*, for all dynamic energy when forcibly compressed reaches a high state of tension. The process that goes on in the construction of Beethoven's forms is essentially the breaking through of purely dynamic forces. These forces no longer represent merely the movement of melodically and harmonically active tones. The music now moves in quick, impetuous outbursts, in waves of increasing and lessening volume, in passionate expressions, in sudden contrasts. While the elements conducive to such forms of expression sprang from the very nature of harmonic music, only a profoundly passionate nature like Beethoven could have carried them to fulfillment. The two things hang together, and with them a third factor—the representation of *poetic ideas*—now enters into the structure of form. Not that Beethoven arbitrarily set out to interpret some particular experience in music. The process is rather an organic continuation of harmonic instrumental form. I have just said that in Beethoven's hands the substance of music undergoes condensation, compression. In the same measure expression both as a whole and in detail becomes intensified. It is like the continuous diminishing of a picture projected upon a wide screen, where the lines of the features grow more and more distinct until what first appeared merely as a head proves at a given point to be the portrait of an individual.

This condensation brings about intensified emotional effects, which in turn relate to the expression of a fundamental idea behind the music. Music is no longer sonority pure and simple; it contains abstract ideas. Beethoven did not write music to preconceived ideas, but the ideas and the music went inseparably together. With him, the dynamic urge which is an organic part of all harmonic music, goes far beyond the ordinary scope of dynamic impulses and becomes the means of interpreting an idea. He does not picture this idea in the programmatic sense; it is the *acting dynamic principle* of the music. As such it is indispensable to him. In the "Eroica" Symphony, the "Farewell" Sonata, the quartet movement entitled "The Difficult Resolve" and many other compositions, he frankly states his idea. At other times he merely indicates it by *interpretation marks*. These interpretation marks, or dynamic indications, which Beethoven uses with a freedom and a diversity of meaning heretofore unknown, are not mere technical instructions but allusions to the fundamental idea in the music.

All this seems so obvious as not to need mention. But an attempt is being made at present to deny that Beethoven's music bore any relation to ideas, to deny, that is, its essentially ideal character. One might say that Michelangelo's "Moses" represents a man seated, holding two tablets, having energetic features and two horns upon his head; but it would be more to the point to recognize the *idea* of Moses as a vital and inalienable part of the statue which we cannot dismiss without doing it violence. It is just as impossible to dismiss the idea from Beethoven's music without misrepresenting the man. It is the idea which constitutes the constructive power, the dynamic principle of form in his compositions. It is the idea which determines the character of his work and which makes possible the further development of harmonic music.

Beethoven's true relationship with Schiller and Kant lies in their all being men who stood for ideas, though they worked along different creative lines. But in his particular type of ideas Beethoven is the great child of a great imaginative era—an era in which the gods and heroes of idealism throve, an era which believed in man as a spiritual being, in freedom and brotherhood, in the joy of divine inspiration, in the everlasting peace and happiness of mankind.

Whatever we may think of these notions today, they did once exist, they were a reality in the spiritual life of the time, and this we must realize in seeking to understand that life. Then we shall also understand how it was that harmonic instrumental music and no other became the medium for the enunciation of such ideas. The voice would never have been suitable, its tone being dependent on physiological factors, on sex and on language. But the instrument has no sex character, it is independent of words and of vocal utterance. Instrumental tone is capable, therefore, of *interpreting the abstract,* and it possesses dynamic potentialities far beyond the scope of the human voice.

Thus Beethoven, like Haydn, is principally a composer of *instrumental* music. His vocal compositions are influenced through and through by an instrumental conception, and they stress, moreover, the cooperation of instruments with the voice in a previously unaccustomed manner. In "Fidelio," his only opera, the subject matter alone is an idea, the glorification of self-sacrificing love, of a soul set free. We shall never fail to feel the ideal significance of his symphonies, his sonatas, his chamber music, save when we hear them no more. Almost everything Beethoven wrote is still alive, still our immediate spiritual possession. It set a stamp upon the musical life of the whole succeeding century. The programs of regular orchestral concerts all over the world center about a Beethoven symphony. Until Beethoven's day public concerts had been exceptional, for art was not thought of as a public matter as it is today. Where music was performed in public it served some special purpose, with Bach the church, with Haydn entertainment. Opera as a public function was only in its beginnings, particularly in Germany, and even here music was subservient to the stage.

But now came music that was performed and listened to for its own sake, a thing which would never have come about had not music now contained within itself something which justified its existence over and above its mere sonorousness. This was the power of expressing ideas, a quality not all music possesses but which is the particular characteristic of this music. It exerted a unifying influence from which a new community evolved, *the musical public*. In this light, Beethoven's music, though secular in form, must be considered as essentially *cult* music. As such it exerts a unifying influence similar to that exercised during the first ten centuries after Christ by the Gregorian chant, during a later period by the music of the Netherlands, and during the 17th century by Italian opera.

This art, addressed to all mankind, embraces all mankind in the depths of its humanity. It includes every sort of music yet created, folk music and church music, the music of entertainment and of opera. It is music which in every sense belongs to the age of "the Enlightenment," an art which scrutinizes all authority, every conventional belief, recognizing only the law man carries in his own breast. It comes to represent a new religion, of belief in an idea, the idea of a great and free humanity. In this sense all the music of the 18th century, the music of Bach and Handel, of Gluck and Haydn, of Mozart and Beethoven, is one.

CHAPTER XVI

EARLY ROMANTICISM—WEBER AND SCHUBERT

THE German classical period is the last in which we find a unifying cult music. With the death of Goethe and Beethoven this period comes to an end. What happened before now happens again. There is a splitting up into national groups, emphasis is laid no longer upon universality but upon national distinctiveness. This new attitude is called *Romanticism*. It intensifies the subjective element in classical idealism, stressing what is actually unique in the individual. It sets forth to give expression to those particular qualities only which happen to determine the characteristics of a personality. But in so doing, it seeks to impress everything else with this same unique stamp. It is the impossibility of realizing such an illusory aim that leads to the tragical mood, the pessimistic temper of this age in which passionate, surging conflicts, dissatisfaction with life, resignation, flight from the world, and retreat into the solitude of self, are characteristic symptoms. A critical *intellectual* and *psychological* attitude is responsible for these conditions

Born at Eutin in Holstein 1786.   died in London Monday June the 5th 1826.

and manifests itself in art by making possible a new intensity of dynamic impulses. Herein lies the new creative stimulus in music.

The disintegration into separate national expressions of forces which had been held together by the cult of the ideal is characteristic of earlier similar processes. The catastrophic *rapidity* of the decay in this case, however, is astonishing. The absence of any opposition shows that the religion of "the Enlightenment"—the belief in the idea—was, even more than orthodox religion, the work of man. Based on intellect alone, it lacked the uniting corporeal strength which the church possesses in its dogma, a body of beliefs which may help men to weather spiritual crises and itself gain new strength in the process. Belief in ideas was bound to go under the moment the intellect itself failed. This process began while Schiller was still alive, at the turn of the 19th century, during the first quarter of which it proceeded with such rapidity that Goethe and Beethoven, reaching over into the new century, seemed almost like relics of the old. With their death, romanticism held undisputed sway.

Goethe, Schiller, Mozart, and even Gluck and Haydn, indeed, already showed certain elements of the romantic, for romanticism, having been born of classicism, must have been contained within it. But it is Beethoven who points the way to romanticism most clearly in his ruthless individualism, in the stress he lays upon the symbolic significance of music and upon its power of expression—that is, upon all its dynamic values. With him, however, these are but means of expressing an impersonal unifying idea; the emphasizing of the particular is never an end in itself, but points toward the larger aspect of the universal. The structure of the Ninth Symphony, crowned by the Ode to Joy, is in this respect a model of the classical attitude in art, in which romantic egotism is transformed into a broad human spirit. The romantic composer would have brought this symphony to a close not with a chorus expressing joy but with some form of self-glorification. Thus Goethe's words relate as much to Beethoven as to himself: "The classical I call healthy, and the romantic sick. Most of the new is romantic not because it is new but because it is weak, sickly and infirm, and the old is classical not because it is old, but because it is strong, fresh, joyous and healthy." Goethe is not differentiating here between the classic and romantic *styles*. He is describing the emphasis upon the *pathological* as characteristic of romanticism, and he calls it weak and sick. Yet all 19th century art was influenced by this very quality. So that after all Goethe's definition does apply in a general way to the classic and romantic styles in art, as he, the classical genius, inevitably saw them.

It is difficult for us to speak of the art of the 19th century. We have reached a point today where we are as well aware as Goethe was of the pathological character which he thought fundamental to romanticism, and feel the same objection toward it. This was not true of the 19th century, where this pathological quality, on the contrary, was considered indispensable to the creation of works of art. Inasmuch as we are turning away from it, back from exaggeration of the particular toward fundamental general types, we necessarily assume a *critical* attitude toward the 19th century, the attitude of sons toward their fathers. This attitude is unavoidable where two periods follow each other in such close succession, and it is justified in so far as it indicates an urge toward continued productivity and is not meant to be deprecatory. But there is some danger lest, on account of our opposing point of view, we look less objectively at this time and its people than at earlier times; just as the generation after 1750, because of its easily comprehensible opposition to the contrapuntal style, failed to do full justice to Bach and Handel, while with the appearance of harmonic melody about 1600, the polyphonic composers were very critically handled.

This sort of antagonism, therefore, while easily explained and forgiven on human grounds, is apt to create a wrong point of view of which we should beware in our present study. As children of the 19th century and grandchildren of the 18th, we find our grandparents more sympathetic than our parents. Our children will perhaps think differently.

The element in romanticism which we call pathological will no longer strike them as so disturbing. Already most of us find a composition like Wagner's "Tristan" very clear, transparent and smooth in form. Our whole power of perception changes also, as we saw in the case of Mozart and his music. What in its own time seems wild and irregular may be considered artistic, well balanced and pleasing a century later. We have not yet arrived at this more mature attitude with regard to the 19th century, being still somewhat antagonistic towards it. I shall therefore avoid entering into a detailed discussion of its music as it would entail a special sort of criticism.

In the next four chapters, accordingly, I shall simply give a general survey of the main currents in romanticism up to the end of the 19th century, and in the last chapter I shall try to describe the approximate status of musical conditions at the present time.

In the beginning I differentiated between two kinds of music, *cult* music and *secular* music. One of the two always dominates: cult music in times of a universal spiritual culture, secular music in times of divergent spiritual tendencies. The 19th century is one of disparity in every field. It is an age without religion, even an irreligious age, and therefore an age of secular music. Church music exists but it is secular in character. Neither religion nor philosophy is able to create a community of interest. Instead

there appears an influence which is an unknown
quantity and scarcely to be defined, in the *public
character* which now attends all musical activity.
This constitutes a purely utilitarian social bond.
It provides two outlets for the 19th century composer, the opera house and the concert hall, and
through these he writes for the public interest.
No other sphere any longer exists for his activity.
The music of the 19th century is thus entirely secular;
it is either opera or concert music. The composer
may awaken or make use of that universal appeal
which is characteristic of the cult, but even so the
cult spirit is confined to expression in the secular
forms of opera or concert music.

Both concert and opera music are stamped with
the creative individuality of the composer. The whole
character of musical style, indeed, is now determined
by this individual quality. Romanticism as a whole
we have seen to be a process of disintegration, developing the psychological to a pathological degree
and setting up an individualistic ethical attitude in
its philosophy. A corresponding process takes place in
romantic music. The harmonic complex splits up
under the influence of intellectual and psychological
tendencies. The chord is reduced to atoms, as it were,
and the active elements of harmony become finer,
more delicately ramified. The tendency toward disintegration, toward diffusion from within, more and
more takes the place of centralized activity. It is ex-

pressed in composition in the increased use of *modulation* and of *chromatics,* and in a corresponding diffusion of *tonal color.* Melody itself now becomes only a part of the whole harmonic activity of tone and color. While the active impulse lay with Bach and Handel in the basses, and with the later classic composers in the melody, it is now concentrated in the middle voices. Harmony breaks up from within, as it were, is forced asunder. Not only is melody swept away in this whirl of tone colors produced by modulation; the importance of the bass in supporting the tonality also vanishes. The composer now bestows all his attention upon modulation and variety of tone color. To him, harmony is the continuous play of consonant tones and the orchestra makes possible the amalgamation of all available tone colors. The development of these two factors in concert and opera music constitutes the main contribution of the 19th century.

I have said that Beethoven and Goethe seemed almost like spirits of the 18th century carried over into the 19th. They are the rivets that bind the two centuries, that hold classicism and romanticism together. The rise of romantic music actually took place under Beethoven's very eyes. When Beethoven died, Spohr had already written his two most famous operas, "Faust" and "Jessonda," and Mendelssohn his overture to "A Midsummer Night's Dream," Marschner was about to compose his "Vampire" and "The

Templar and the Jewess," and Berlioz was working at his "Phantastic Symphony." And of the two leading figures in early romantic music, *Carl Maria von Weber* had died at the age of forty, one year before Beethoven, while *Franz Schubert,* who was eleven years younger than Weber, died only one year after Beethoven. So we may say that the first two great romantic composers in the field of opera and concert had completed their life's work just as Beethoven finished his, while their successors had practically reached their highest achievement at the time of Beethoven's death.

At the mention of Weber, we think first only of his "Freischütz," which, biographically speaking, is of course hardly accurate. Weber wrote several other operas, of which "Euryanthe" and "Oberon" are still performed. He also wrote a considerable number of instrumental compositions, largely for his own use as a piano virtuoso. Some of his songs, furthermore, have passed into the class of popular melodies. Yet for posterity "Der Freischütz" is still Weber's *great* work. It occupies a place of its own in German opera. Not only are all Weber's excellences happily displayed here and all his weaknesses at their least noticeable. "Der Freischütz" signifies more than the composition of an opera; it is Weber's great *cultural* contribution. Despite the "Abduction from the Seraglio," "The Magic Flute" and "Fidelio," "Der Freischütz" is the first *German* opera, German in the new sense, which means that it is limited by national characteristics but at the same time inspired with the young romanticism of this new age. "Der Freischütz" was not only an opera in the German tongue, it was an opera of the German people. In its story it characterised their most intimate feelings, and in form it went back to the old German song-play, being in the main an apotheosis of folk-song, or at least of song in the folk manner. For these reasons, and not for any outstanding artistic quality in Weber himself, "Der Freischütz" achieved a success sensational to a degree we can scarcely imagine nowadays. With it national opera triumphed for the German public. It was the battering-ram which shattered the hold of Spontini, the Italian, who was then general musical director in Berlin, and of Italian opera in Dresden.

The real folk quality of "Der Freischütz" lies in the naturalness and simplicity of the music and the combination of gaiety, sentiment and phantasy in the text. It acquires its particular musical character from the picturesque treatment of orchestral color, as in the wood-wind and horn effects, and from the contrasting of unadorned and simple solo parts with the Huntsmen's and Bridesmaids' choruses. The exalted lyric types of Max and Agatha, the roguish Aennchen, the evil figures of Caspar and Samiel, with the descriptive music of the huntsmen's carousel at the village inn, of the ravine of the wolves, of forest scenes by night and by day—all these features bespeak the

FR. SCHUBERT

geb. den 19ten Nov. 1815.

establishment of a fundamentally German type of opera. Germans everywhere, from city or countryside, were enchanted by its faithful reflection of their own inner life. The typically German character is represented to perfection, as the Italian character is in Rossini's "Barber of Seville" and the French in Bizet's "Carmen." With "Der Freischütz" German romantic opera was not only established but also strictly defined. Weber himself was never able to step beyond the confines here laid down, and those who came after him simply developed certain details more particularly, like Spohr and Marschner, or, like Wagner, expanded into an entirely new field.

As Weber created German romantic opera, so Schubert created German romantic *concert music*. A school-master and teacher of music living in Vienna, he was over-shadowed by the gigantic figure of Beethoven, for which reason his contemporaries and successors scarcely knew him as an instrumental composer. In the beginning his fame was founded on the *Lied*, a type of composition which had been comparatively little cultivated. If German romantic opera never went beyond Weber's "Freischutz," a like situation holds good with regard to Schubert's songs. Both the sacred or spiritual and the secular or social forms of the Lied may be traced back to the minnesingers. The music, being set to the verse form of the Lied, was naturally dependent upon the literary level of the day. Among Schubert's predecessors

and contemporaries, who wrote songs of this type in
which the music was an aid to the poetry, the Berlin
school in particular, with Peter Abraham Schultz,
Reichardt and Zelter, is worthy of note. But the
romantic Lied, being a musical composition to a certain extent independent of the poem, presupposed
that subjective quality in musical expression which
first appeared in the post-classical period. This form
of the Lied was indeed the most original, the most independent, the finest creation of romantic music.
Here all the romantic elements converged in a great
art form which could only have come into being with
the fulfillment of all the possibilities inherent in these
elements. Here, too, intensified individuality found
its most direct and ideal form of expression. While the
classical composers had been but incidentally interested in the Lied, Schubert, the first great romanticist, was also the first to voice the new type of self-
expression in this form.

   As an instrumental composer, too, Franz Schubert
determined the general tendencies of the 19th century. Only superficially do his symphonies, his chamber works, his piano music, seem to stand on the same
foundations as Beethoven's. Their structure is in
reality determined by the two fundamental characteristics of romantic music, the activity of modulation
inherent in the harmony and the stressing of *color
sense*. These break up the severe organic unity of
Beethoven's forms, with their singleness of idea, into

a multiplicity of episodes, fantastic pictures, romantic reveries. Beethoven's monumental massiveness dissolves, gives place to a complexity of lyric detail. The strength of the single idea gives way to the charm of variety, of kaleidoscopic change, of fantastic visions. Thus vanishes the heroic age. The individual human being with his particular joys and sorrows stands alone before the world, and music becomes the medium for expressing his own consciousness, the voice of his own experience.

CHAPTER XVII

NATIONAL ROMANTICISM IN CONCERT AND OPERA

In saying that romantic music voiced the composer's own experience, I do not mean to imply that the composers of the romantic period had experiences different from their predecessors, which they proceeded to interpret directly in their art. We may assume that experience is the same for all men at all times; only the forms of experience are modified under the influence of different cultures. The significance of experience for *art* is another matter. An attitude which considers the particular as but a transitory phase naturally attaches little importance to the experiences of the individual, and regards them merely as means to the understanding of the whole. An attitude, on the other hand, which sees the general typified in the particular must tend to intensify the capacity for experience in the individual. It must take experiences themselves seriously because they reflect life and the world as a whole. In short, it is not the experience that is new, but the significance that is attributed to it.

When we say that art expresses experience, people

usually think that the artist goes through some sort
of human trial, a love affair or a great sorrow, and
so acquires an idea for a work of art. This notion
seems to be confirmed by Goethe's words:

"And when Man in his anguish grows mute
A God it is gives words to tell the pain,"

and by Heine also when he says:

"Out of my great, great sorrow
I make my little songs."

But we should beware of so interpreting these lines,
lest we confound cause and effect. A work of art does
not grow out of an experience, is not the result of
accidental circumstances. The desire to create always
comes first and it is the creative urge which *impels*
the necessary experience. With the increased importance of individual experience in the new romantic
attitude, the composer's whole life is forced into the
service of his art. He has to induce his own adventures in joy and sorrow in order to bring to light the
work that is latent within him. Bach did not need to
bring experience thus directly into his composing;
he could outwardly lead the life of a worthy citizen
without harming his art. But as the creative process
becomes more and more subjective, the personal life
of the composer is *drawn into* it. The influence of
the ideal nature of their art is apparent in the lives
of Mozart and Beethoven; but with the romanticists

the exclusive domination of the subjective leads, as it were, to the opposite extreme. Personality is completely absorbed, swept along in the creative process. It almost ceases to exist on its own account in becoming the end and aim of artistic expression.

Romantic art now passes into a new phase. Through an excessive subjectivism it reduces real human values to naught and becomes a theatrical art. In regarding man as but an instrument for the accomplishment of artistic ends, in setting the resistless urge of the individual creative spirit above life itself, it robs that life of its value. Thus romanticism comes to *overrate* art. And art is no longer an elevating influence, no longer a bearer of the joy and the deeper awareness of living. It becomes an end in itself, a law unto itself, a fount of all understanding, a religion. This holds true in varying degrees with romantic artists everywhere.

The national characteristics in romantic art were also connected with this urge toward expression of personal experience, for in them the artist found his nearest medium for a fuller individual expression. Thus we see how the music of the 19th century increasingly divides into national schools. In the first half of the century Germany, France and Italy are the leading musical nations. In the second half, the Scandinavians branch out independently, the Russians, the Czechs, the English, the Spanish, the Americans, and the divisions and subdivisions become always more numerous. The process goes hand in hand

with political developments, and is still active today. It is impossible to take up each of these national
branches here, and we shall therefore only attempt to
indicate the main tendencies and to mention some of
the most outstanding personalities.

I have said that opera and concert music were the
two fundamental types of romantic composition and
that Weber and Schubert were the first German representatives of these forms. Contemporaneously with
these two, and also immediately after them, a number
of kindred composers appeared in Germany, France
and Italy. Though they differed from each other in-
dividually, they had in common the tendency to
deviate from the unifying aspirations of classical art
and to accentuate national characteristics. In opera,
as "Der Freischütz" showed, this was evident in the
choice and treatment of subject matter. In concert
music, apart from the Lied which remained an essentially German form, national character could not be
so obviously expressed in subject matter, but it appeared, nevertheless, in diversity of form and in the
varied development of instrumental technique and
expression. This last was the contribution of the
virtuosi who now appeared upon the scene—German,
French, Polish, Spanish, Belgian, Norwegian, English,
Italian—violin or piano players for the most part.
Among these virtuosi two came to the fore whose influence in music history was far-reaching, *Paganini*
and *Liszt.*

We incline today to underrate the cultural significance of virtuosity because we know it only as a re-
productive activity. True virtuosity, however, as
represented by Paganini and Liszt, is creative. It expresses itself in *improvisation,* where all effects are
concentrated upon the moment of performance,
to which end all the charms of instrumental tone
are exploited. It was in these fanciful revelations that
the fascination of virtuoso playing, its magic effect
upon the listeners, lay. Technical dexterity was a
secondary matter and was first intentionally practiced
when the virtuoso no longer improvised but exhibited
his skill in some given composition. If a violinist plays
the Paganini Caprices today, that is in itself an accomplishment, for they are among the most difficult
compositions in violin literature. But even the most
perfect reproduction is not to be compared with
Paganini's own playing of them. The remarkable
thing was not that Paganini could play these pieces
but that he was the first to make such pieces possible.
The extraordinary effect, the ecstatic transports that
gripped people when they heard him play, were
caused by his revealing of possibilities in the instrument which had never been dreamed of. Paganini's
violin gave voice to the spirit of romanticism itself,
individual, subjective, displaying all the dynamic
forces of the music, all the expressive nuances of a
singing tone, all the characteristic color of the instrument.

What Paginini did for the violin, Liszt did for the piano. He called attention to all its possibilities of modulation and color, reformed piano-playing, in other words, in accord with the specific characteristics of romantic style. Liszt was not unique. Chopin, the Pole, was very like him; also Hummel and Thalberg, who belonged, respectively, to the older and younger generations of Mozart's pupils. But Liszt had the widest range of interest of them all. Not satisfied with the piano alone, he proceeded to transmit to the *orchestra* all that he had learned from it in the way of modulation and color effects.

The romantic orchestra was an outgrowth of this same stimulus of virtuosity. It was first developed in France by *Berlioz,* who very much resembled Liszt. Berlioz was also a virtuoso, but from the very outset his instrument was the orchestra. Like Liszt, he was profoundly influenced by Paganini; but he carried the inspiration into his compositions, and here Beethoven was his model. With Berlioz, Beethoven's spiritual idea is changed into the realistic *programmatic* idea, which now becomes the leading thought in the virtuoso orchestra. The programmatic idea is strictly personal, self-revelatory. The composer himself, the subjective quality of the idea he expresses in his program, takes the place of the actual instrumental virtuoso. The program is an idealized personal expression, so to speak. Here lies the difference between the old, purely pictorial program music and romantic program music, which is the exposition of personal experience, of an individual interpretation.

In their leaning toward the programmatic idea, which aimed to achieve the utmost brilliance of orchestral harmony and color, Berlioz and Liszt were alike. But they put the idea to different uses. With Berlioz, the Frenchman, it was always associated with the visual, with action, as in the opera; while Liszt strove for abstract expression, passing into the realm of thought. Hence Liszt's inclination toward the German romanticism of Mendelssohn and Schumann and, in particular, of Schubert.

German instrumental music also was influenced by the stimulus of virtuosity, the real significance of which was the rôle it played as a means of developing expression. Music became a *tone-language* in which *emotional experience* was interpreted in poetic form. Characteristic examples are to be found in Mendelssohn's "Songs Without Words" and in his overtures to "A Midsummer Night's Dream," "Fingal's Cave," "Calm Sea and Prosperous Voyage," and in certain piano works of Schumann, the "Davidsbündler Dances," "Kreisleriana," "Carnival," "Scenes of Childhood." The poetic idea was taken for granted as the inspiration and setting for the music. Schumann's writings give us to understand that to him the inner relation between music and poetic experience was beyond question. But the German romanticists showed no liking for the naturalistic interpretation of Berlioz

nor the breadth of form for which Liszt strove. Their
art was simple, inclining towards the intimate, the
contemplative. Hence their preference for smaller
chamber music forms and for the Lied or part-songs.
They even treated the orchestra with a view less to
full and glowing color than to the display of delicate
pastel shades. They avoided great pathos in favor of a
gentle, pleasant spirit of revery. This tendency to *in-
trospection*, to absorption in their own dream-world,
was peculiar to the German romantic composers.

Individuals differed, of course. Mendelssohn's form
is notable for the clearness of construction, the polish
and symmetry which characterise him as the most
classical of the romanticists. Schumann's, on the other
hand, is typical for its unevenness, its breaking up
of outline, its fantastic spirit overflowing here and
fading there. The lives of these two composers corresponded with their natures. Mendelssohn, passing
from success to success as a piano virtuoso and
founder of modern orchestral conducting, died at
the height of his activities, celebrated everywhere as
a leading composer. Schumann, who had a long struggle for the recognition which he was never un-
stintingly accorded, became mentally deranged. It is a
strange coincidence, perhaps not unconnected with
the type of music they wrote, that the four greatest
of the early German romanticists—Weber, Schubert,
Mendelssohn and Schumann—died young, or at least
did their best work in early life. They were all chil-

dren of spring. Their physical constitution lasted only until early manhood. Where, as with Schumann, it endured longer, the mind wearied and at last gave out.

The same holds good for the German romantic opera composers, inasmuch as their main works were written during the first half of their lives. *Spohr* was only fourteen years younger than Beethoven. A violinist of the grand style, he represents German romantic virtuosity at its height. He is remembered, apart from his violin concertos, especially for his operas "Faust" and "Jessonda." But in his own time he also had far-reaching influence as a composer of symphonies and oratorios, and being a conductor, he belongs, like Mendelssohn, among the practical organizers of public musical life. *Heinrich Marschner,* who was nine years Weber's junior, devoted himself to conducting and composing when still young. His great successes were "Vampire," "The Templar and the Jewess," and "Hans Heiling" which appeared in 1833, all written before his fortieth year. Marschner and Weber have some traits in common; for example, the popular vein and forms of their music, and the leaning towards the fantastic, which with Marschner rises to the gruesome, the uncanny, and leads to new harmonies and color combinations. Spohr, on the other hand, is primarily the lyric spirit, the composer of ingeniously melodious music. But he lacks the robust folk-style, especially in his rhythm, and therewith the direct simplicity of the popular manner. His "Jessonda" is noteworthy for its leaning toward the exotic, expressed in the play of chromatics and an unusual treatment of color.

Italian and French opera ran parallel with German opera in their own definite national strains. In discussing opera before Gluck's time, I pointed out that the most characteristically Italian type was the opera buffa. This form was just as inimitable, in its way, as the German Lied and the romantic opera of the "Freischütz" type which sprang from it. Such forms can only emanate from a definite national psychology. For this reason, again, their influence is limited. Thus we can scarcely picture the real charm of opera buffa properly unless we hear it sung by Italians in Italian. This type, which various composers had brought to universal recognition in the second half of the 18th century, reached its height in Rossini's "Barber of Seville," first performed in 1816. Rossini was then twenty-four years old. He had begun composing at sixteen and continued until he was thirty-seven, when he definitely concluded his career as an operatic composer with "William Tell." He lived almost forty years longer, but wrote only small piano pieces and a few religious works, among them the famous "Stabat Mater." Thus it happened with Rossini as it happened with the German romanticists: his productive power ceased towards the end of his fourth decade. His younger contemporary, *Bellini*, who was famous especially for his wealth of melody, lived to be only thirty-four years old, while *Donizetti,* the third of this generation of Italians, like Schumann, suffered a mental breakdown on the threshold of his fortieth year.

With these three Italians of the first third of the 18th century, Italian opera, both seria and buffa, was carried on in undiminished freshness. The operas of the great Italianized Germans, Gluck and Mozart, were not considered nationally characteristic. Mozart's operas, indeed, always met with least response in Italy. The Italian is always a singer, whether in comic or in tragic mood; he *sings* and derives dramatic form from the laws of singing alone. For this reason the works of Rossini, Bellini and Donizetti show no important difference in form from those of the 18th century. They simply absorbed into the realm of vocal expression the stimulus derived from virtuosity in instrumental music. The voice continued to dominate until the middle of the century when a new master, *Giuseppe Verdi,* appeared, who, fusing the art of his three predecessors and reaching beyond the idea of *bel canto,* gave to the singing voice the natural human quality of individual expression.

In France *opera comique* and grand opera offered a contrast similar to that of opera seria and opera buffa in Italy. Opera comique was the expression of popular sentiment, while grand opera stood primarily for dramatic representation. Hence the individuality

of French art is more striking and more characteristic in opera comique. In the operas of Adam, Auber,
Méhul, Boieldieu and many others, we have a long
list of pleasing and delightful examples of typically
French art. In these the work of the smaller composers
of the 18th century—Monsigny, Philidor, Grétry—
is carried over into its romantic phase. Founded on
the fundamental forms of the lyric *chanson* and the
metrical *couplet,* opera comique is the French representative of the German song-play.

The less intimate *grand opera,* with its rhetorical
pathos and dramatic emotion, was not intended to
be particularly national in character or subject-
matter. Many of the composers who wrote in this
form were themselves not French. Gluck was a German. After him came the Italians Cherubini, Spontini
and, after Auber's great success with "La Muette de
Portici," Rossini with his "William Tell." The French-
men, Méhul, Halévy, Hérold, naturally turned to
grand opera as well as to opera comique, but they
were all outstripped by the German, Jacob Meyer
Beer, or, as he later called himself, *Giacomo Meyerbeer.* In his operas, of which "Robert le Diable," "les
Huguenots," "le Prophète" and "l'Africaine" still
live, virtuosity triumphs. The rôles are written for
singers who are both highly trained virtuosi and con-
summate actors. The decorative setting demands ex-
pert handling of technical apparatus, and Meyerbeer's
treatment of the orchestra reveals him as an instru-

mental composer ranking with Berlioz in skill, while his wealth of melody shows an inventiveness equal to that of the Italians. He is one of the ablest composers in the history of music, the type that masters everything, knows everything, does everything correctly, and has at his command both taste and an unerring instinct. Thus he was one of the greatest, even among all the virtuosi of his time—the Paganini, Liszt and Berlioz of opera, the great composer-virtuoso. In this capacity he conquered from Paris the stages of the world until he was succeeded by another, who strove for the same domination and who now precipitated the dramatic wars of the 19th century. This man was *Richard Wagner.*

CHAPTER XVIII

WAGNER, VERDI, BIZET

I HAVE described romanticism as a fundamentally theatrical art, because it strips the life of the individual of its larger human value and makes its more dramatic elements the subject of artistic expression. It seems fitting, therefore, that the greatest representatives of romantic art in the field of music, *Richard Wagner*, the German, and *Giuseppe Verdi*, the Italian, should have been composers of opera, of musical drama. *Georges Bizet*, the Frenchman, ranks with them, for although his work does not compare with theirs in quality and intellectual worth, nevertheless he created in "Carmen" the representative French opera of the second half of the 19th century, clearly contrasting his own national type of opera with Wagner's German and Verdi's Italian types. So long as we are not weighing individual composers on their own account but seeking to point out the nature of certain events in music history, Bizet should be included in this group of leaders of the second half of the century.

The romantic movement in music has been described as a breaking up of the harmonic structure through the activity of modulation and of tone color. Both of these being dynamic processes, we may state the case more simply by saying that what we call the romantic style in music is based upon an increasingly complex conception of dynamics, affecting all the elements of musical construction. The purpose of form, then, is to bring into this dynamic activity an æsthetic order based upon the close relationship of tone effects and the power of expression. The composer perceives tonal activity as symbolic of emotion, which is now distilled down from the universal poetic idea of Beethoven to some particular personal thought. This thought is represented in the definite programs of Liszt and Berlioz, in the lyric mood of Schubert, Mendelssohn and Schumann; in the inspiration behind virtuosity, which is the direct reproduction of personality itself, and in the subject-matter and the structure typical of romantic opera. These expressions are all based on the romantic conception of music as a *language of tones,* a language capable of representing accurately every inner process, every dynamic accent. Like all language, it is not an end in itself but seeks to express something. Romantic music, accordingly, becomes the medium for the expression of something else, something outside the realm of music. This something is an emotion, and from the nature of this emotion the constructive principle of form in romantic music is derived.

It follows that the composer had to find emotional stimulus of every conceivable sort. The fuller the emotional impulses, the richer their contribution to music. The poetic idea, the programmatic idea, the self-portrayal of the virtuoso, provided incentives of this sort. But the strongest and most productive impulse came from the *drama*. Here all the powers of imagination, all self-revelation, all poetic and programmatic ideas mingled together, having a direct influence on music and in turn being influenced by it. For this reason the most robust and virile composers of the romantic movement were irresistibly drawn to the drama. Wagner and Verdi were of this romantic stuff in every respect, even to their physical make-up. We have seen that all the early romanticists died young or wrote their principal compositions in their youth. This was also true of Bizet, but not of Wagner and Verdi. Both were healthy, long-lived, tenacious spirits. Wagner lived to be seventy, Verdi past eighty-seven, and both wrote their best works only after their fortieth years.

Now to sum up briefly the essential characteristics of these three men in the light of what has just been said, I should say that Wagner interprets dramatic impulses, primarily from the *instrumental* point of view, wherein he is the German; Verdi interprets dramatic impulses primarily from the *vocal* point of view, wherein he is the Italian; Bizet interprets dramatic impulses primarily from the point of view

of the *rhythm of the language,* wherein he is the
Frenchman. By carrying this distinction further, we
may clearly picture the individualities of these three
composers as well as the contrasts they present among
themselves.

After "Lohengrin," Wagner no longer called his
works operas. "Tristan" he called a "drama," the
"Ring of the Nibelung" a "festival play" and
"Parsifal" a "sacred festival play for the stage," while
the "Mastersingers" and the separate operas of the
"Ring" have no special designation. Wagner always
vigorously opposed the term "music drama"—without success, to be sure, since he himself could not
think of a suitable name. Yet he paraphrases in his
own words what he considers the characteristic nature
of his works when he calls them *"visible manifestations of music."* This may sound awkward and is
hardly the sort of thing to print on opera programs,
but it is nevertheless the most keen and comprehensive designation, containing Wagner's whole creative
code. It states two of his beliefs: firstly that all tonal
activity—the activity of modulation, of melody and
of rhythmic accents—is a musical "act," a *drama* of
tones and tone-relations; secondly, that the dramatic
action on the stage is the *visible manifestation* of
this tonal activity, the projection of music into visible
scenic form.

To Wagner, in short, tones are the actors, harmony
is the mimetic action, or in other words, the singer

we see on the stage personifies tone and the action represents harmonic activity. This is what Wagner means by his "visible manifestations of music." The dynamic impulses of the action are those of the music, because the music itself expresses the action. Music and drama, or, more precisely harmony and action, are not two different things. They are identical in essence and different only in form. The artistic principle, therefore, lies neither in the action nor in the music, but in an emotional dynamic force which expresses itself on the stage and in the music simultaneously.

Let us make clear this absolute unity of musical form and dramatic idea by an example. We know that Wagner's plots, from "The Flying Dutchman" to "Parsifal," deal again and again with the idea of redemption. The stories, the statements of the problem, vary, but the fundamental idea remains, as it must remain, not because it expresses some philosophic or poetic attitude of Wagner's, but because it is the interpretation in dramatic action of a constantly recurring *organic musical process*. All harmonic music progresses along a certain course, the steps of which are: first, the statement of the fundamental harmony, secondly, the disturbance of this fundamental harmony by a dynamic impetus which destroys its balance, as it were, and thirdly the return of the disturbed tones to the equilibrium of the fundamental harmony. This return is called a *cadence*, the tones coming to rest again in the fundamental harmony. If the composer thinks of this process as a dramatic plot, he welcomes the return of the disturbed tones into the original harmony as a solution, a "redemption." Thus the idea of redemption in Wagner's plots is inherently identical with the idea of cadence in music. As he knows and creates harmonic music only, and as harmonic music must by nature strive irresistibly toward the cadence, Wagner's dramatic action, too, must be a story of redemption.

Here is an example of what I have called "the *drama* of tones and tone-relations," the idea that harmonic activity is conditioned by the dramatic action. This is an idea which can naturally be carried to the most minute detail. It is scarcely necessary to point out that it is characteristic not only of Wagner, but of all romantic composers. There is no romantic opera, therefore, no romantic music, even, which does not express the idea of redemption. Because romantic music is harmonic music which always progresses toward the cadence, and in representing this tendency, romantic music is inevitably made to express the urge towards solution, towards salvation. The difference between Wagner and his predecessors lies merely in the fact that he grasped the relation between dramatic action and harmonic processes with absolute assurance and formulated it distinctly. Thus he blazed for his successors a trail from which they could not stray so long as music still progressed towards a harmonic cadence.

For these reasons, Wagner of necessity laid great stress on the development of the *orchestra*. He needed an apparatus capable of expressing all the possibilities of harmonic activity and of converting them into ever-changing dramatic impulses. From this same dramatic conception of music followed the increased use of chromatics in both melody and harmony which Wagner took over from Liszt, the recognition of melody as but a surface-line of harmony, the constant enriching of color effects after the example of Berlioz and Meyerbeer. To this end, where the orchestra was concerned every stimulus inspired by the virtuoso style served his purposes; in other respects many of the lyric effects introduced by Schubert, Mendelssohn, and Schumann also proved useful. Wagner worked *synthetically* in the highest sense. Italian, German and French opera, Bellini and Donizetti, Weber, Mendelssohn, Schumann, Marschner, Auber, and Meyerbeer above all, furnished him with building material. We must not be misled by his polemics against Schumann and Mendelssohn, against the Italians, and against Meyerbeer's grand opera in particular. They are the expression of revolt against those things which stood nearest him. Not that Wagner's relationship to his predecessors meant that he was outwardly dependent upon them. He possessed the power of assimilating the best of all their different contributions, of absorbing everything that had gone before. Only in this way could he have progressed beyond the delicate and intimate but limited romanticism of Weber and become the great master of musical drama.

I think I have now indicated what is essential for this brief survey—the *change* in tone-perception which is most clearly manifested in Wagner. It is a change to the *visual* conception. Music is now looked upon as the interplay of tonal forces, representing the dramatic activity of emotion. This interpretation goes beyond the idea of the symphonic program and is projected in a visible stage picture. Wagner, the German, expressed this ideal through the medium of the orchestra as the instrument representing harmonic activity. *Verdi*, the Italian, expressed it in the *voice*, in the development of which, as in Wagner's orchestra, all the potential possibilities of harmonic color are now reflected.

It is customary to compare Wagner and Verdi as contrasting types. This is all very well in so far as they distinctly represent the musical characteristics of two great nations. But it is not fair to apply the contrast to the conceptions the two men held of their art. These were, on the contrary, *alike;* only the means of expression each used differed throughout according to their national peculiarities. Just as Wagner goes back to German folk music, so Verdi goes back to Italian folk music. Verdi clung to this origin of his, but tried to keep it only as the nucleus about which all other outside inspirations might gather and crystallize into a larger form. Wagner and Verdi were both affected by French opera, and both experienced the influence of Meyerbeer to which they largely owe their distinctively individual expression. Like Wagner, Verdi develops harmonic possibilities; the development of his forms is based on the expansion of modulation and color. But where with Wagner the dramatic activity of the music centres in the *orchestra,* for which he creates the *leit-motif* technique peculiar to himself, with Verdi, the song-inspired Italian, it is reflected in the *voice.* The treatment of the voice is thus subject, as it were, to the dynamics of modulation and color. Here lay the gradually developing difference between the old Italian opera of Rossini and Bellini, with their bel canto ideal, and the operas of Verdi in which the voice simply and directly expressed natural emotion, outbursts of passionate feeling, and was subject in its development to the harmonic progress of the music. Thus Verdi was the originator of emotional Italian music, passionate—stirring, impetuous, dreamy—the creator of *realistic* melody in contrast to the bel canto. I have just sought to indicate the source from which this realistic music arose. It is the same source as that from which, on German soil, Wagner's symphonic drama grew.

Neither with Wagner nor with Verdi was this a sudden development. Verdi did not theorize, indeed, as Wagner did, but for this difference also only the material of their art and not its nature was responsible. Wagner's theorizing is explained by the complex possibilities which his medium of instrumental harmony offered. But because of the nature of the voice, Verdi could only learn about his material with practice. So that it was always their method only, not the nature of their art, which differed. If Wagner began (in his "Fairies") by imitating Weber and Marschner, Verdi began by imitating Donizetti. From then on their paths ran parallel till they met in Meyerbeer. So we have approximately thirty operas by Verdi, some unjustly neglected, but many of them predestined failures of which not even the names are remembered. They nearly all deal with serious and tragic subjects; indeed, except for one youthful work, Verdi wrote but a single comic opera, "Falstaff," which he finished when almost eighty. This work never became and probably never will become as popular as "Othello" which he wrote five years earlier, in the way, that is, in which Rossini's "Barber of Seville" is popular. Yet it is one of the most delightful and one of the finest achievements of the entire operatic literature, a dispassionate, almost a superhuman creation, written by one who has experienced and so depicted everything life has to offer, and who now stands aside surveying it all, letting the play of desires and emotions dance by in the guise of a comedy.

PORTRAIT DE VERDI

At the end of the 19th century it was usual to regard Verdi as inferior to Wagner, to dismiss him as
a gifted writer of hand-organ music. The opposite
view now prevails and the complex symbolism of
Wagner's instrumental language is deprecated in favor of Verdi's wealth of melody. Errors both. Wagner
and Verdi should be regarded as two trees springing
from the same root and together almost completely
overshadowing the second half of the 19th century.
They are both romanticists, they both bring national
opera into bloom, both reach out from their native
soil and absorb productive elements of nourishment
from all the countries of the world. The life's work
of each is a gigantic monument, the achievement of
a great and rich existence, full of conflict, but ending
with the victory of the *individual*. So they have both
rightly come to be looked upon historically as the
representatives of their people in the second half of
the 19th century, *national heroes,* in their persons and
in their music, in contrast to the great masters of the
18th century who were citizens of the world.

If Verdi is contrasted with Wagner today, *Bizet*
was a victim of the same fate some forty years ago,
when Nietzsche, in his opposition to Wagner, took
"Carmen" as the positive antithesis of everything
Wagnerian. But the comparison is here still less ap-
propriate than in the case of Verdi. Nietzsche's partiality for everything Gallic or Latin, for the smooth
formality, the wit and vivacity of French music,

made him see in "Carmen" an utter contrast to Wagner's operas, whereas it really represented the same type of thing—the perfect example of a national opera, French, in Bizet's case, as in Verdi's it was Italian. The underlying principles are the same as in Wagner's operas, only they are carried out in characteristic French fashion.

In the first half of the century these French characteristics had been united in *opera comique*, so called not because of the subject-matter, which was lyrical and not comic at all, but because of its contrast to the solemn pathos of grand opera. It was based on the *chanson* and the *couplet*, song-forms in the construction of which the language took an important part, its rhythmic vitality being especially prominent. For this reason the dramatic element became an important part of French opera, the whole structure of which tended to enhance the power of the dramatic action. Precision of form, a pregnant finesse of condensed lyric effects, the absence of all vocalistic display, but also of any symphonic breadth, the absolute concentration of singing, action and orchestra upon the portrayal of the actual dramatic scene—these were all required by the nature of French music. They were ideally carried out in "Carmen." Bizet was quite as much influenced by psychology as Wagner, as the thematic development of his score shows. He was quite as much a realist in his melody as Verdi, as we see in his subordination of melodic line to emotional expression. He was quite as much a romanticist as both of them, as his use of Spanish color in the instrumentation and his stressing of the emotional in action and music shows. But psychology, realism, romanticism, are here never an end in themselves. They are always controlled and moulded by the Frenchman's untiring capacity for rounding any emotion into smooth and fluent form. The form is here imposed by the rhythm of the French language, and it is in the vitality of this rhythm derived from the language, that the power of Bizet's music lies, while that of Verdi's lies in the emotional quality of the melody, and that of Wagner's in the orchestral harmony.

Thus Bizet's "Carmen" is a third type of national opera, apparently less different in structure from the Verdian than from the Wagnerian type. Mussorgski's "Boris Godunov," which was written at the same time as "Carmen," should also be mentioned; but this representative Russian opera becomes significant only for the succeeding generation. National forces have reached their fullest expression and now begin to disintegrate and intermingle, giving birth in France and Italy, following Bizet and Verdi, to the so-called *veristic* movement, in Germany to the postromantic music drama. These movements influence the forms of concert music as well, which now develop into great importance.

CHAPTER XIX

LATE ROMANTICISM IN CONCERT AND OPERA

IN our discussion of Wagner, all romantic music was described as expressing the idea of solution, of redemption, a fundamental characteristic traceable to the fact that all harmonic music moves toward resolution in the cadence. By the same token *pre*-romantic music, in so far as it is harmonic, might be said to express the same idea. In a sense it does. Only the intensity of the suspense, the way in which the forces progressing towards the cadence are handled, is different. With Bach and Handel, where the bass is the leading voice, the relief of the cadence comes less as the resolution of tones in a high state of tension than as a *confirmation* of the sense of harmonic equilibrium. With the classical masters of the Viennese school, where the melody dominates and there is the upward tendency to resolution of the leading tone, the cadence becomes a powerful dynamic development, an outburst of repressed tone-forces, a *climax*. With the romanticists, harmonic activity is centered neither in the basses nor in the melody but in the inner voices, and because of the increased pos-

sibilities of modulation accompanying this dispersion
of harmonic activity from within, the stress of dis-
sonant tension is such that the cadence comes as a
supreme resolution, expressive of a sense of *redemption*. In this intensification of effect lies the essentially *dramatic* character of romantic music, the
greatest works of which, accordingly, deal with the
stage.

This dramatic element had much to do also with
the shaping of the concert forms of romantic music,
although there was, in fact, a constant give and take
between the dramatic and the concert types which
makes it difficult to say with certainty which first
influenced the other. This close interaction explains
the relation between opera and program music, between Wagner, Berlioz and Liszt, and again between
these three and the early German romanticists. Two
different forms developed from the *intensity of expression* characteristic of romantic music. The one
tended toward *expansion,* to elaborate and work up
this expressive quality to the point where it should
directly interpret action and emotion. This was the
direction taken by Berlioz, Liszt and Wagner, which
led to the opera and program music of the so-called
"new German school." The other form was more *intensive.* Here the composer shunned direct interpretation as superficial, and thought dramatic and programmatic ideas should not govern the music entirely
but should merely accompany it. This was the move-

ment which followed hard upon early romanticism
in Germany, and its most important representative
was *Johannes Brahms.* Twenty years younger than
Wagner, Brahms was heir to the early romanticists,
Schubert, Mendelssohn and Schumann, much as
Wagner was heir to the old masters of opera. With
Brahms appeared two other composers whose talents
were highly specialized, *Hugo Wolf,* in the field of
Lieder, and *Anton Bruckner,* in the field of large
symphonic forms. But Wolf and Bruckner were both
very much influenced by Wagner and antagonistic
to Brahms.

We should take note of the dissension that existed
between these two groups surrounding Wagner and
Brahms, unjustified though it seems today. In the
partisan quarrels and newspaper controversies of the
time they were represented as standing one for true,
the other for spurious music, a distinction which of
course seems to us entirely irrelevant. And yet we
should not go so far as to deny all distinctions
between the two groups. The emotional romantic
conception of music is common to both Brahms
and Wagner, but they develop it in entirely different
ways, the one through a process of expansion, the
other through a process of concentration. The difference between the two may be compared to the difference between Handel and Bach, though it relates
only to their manner of composing, not to their
musical individuality. It is reflected in their choice of

medium. Wagner, with his desire to express emotion concretely turns, like Handel, to the drama, while Brahms, with his tendency to abstract emotional expression, turns, like Bach, to instrumental music not connected with drama. Thus Brahms wrote instrumental music of every sort, and with voice as well, but he always kept aloof from opera.

Brahms' relation to the early concert romanticists resembles Wagner's relation to the early romantic opera composers in another way as well. Like Wagner, Brahms surpassed all his predecessors in virility of nature, both in physical strength and in energy of character. He also lived longer, reaching the age of sixty-four, and did most of his best work in the second half of his life. Unlike the youthful early romanticists, he came to a late maturity. These physical differences have an important bearing upon the characteristic creative activity of the individual.

Though he wrote instrumental music of all types, Brahms' main achievement lies in the field of *chamber music*. I mean by this not that his best works are those expressly written for chamber ensemble, but that all his writing has the character of chamber music. This is a structural characteristic. We have seen that the basic feature of romantic style is the dispersion of harmonic activity from the inner voices, which gives rise to great variety of modulation and color. Where this process turned not to the visual or programmatic interpretation of Berlioz, Liszt and

Wagner, but to the concentration of dynamic expression as with Brahms, the composer of necessity renounced any external grandeur of style. This was the natural consequence of the tendency toward subtile diversification, towards an increasingly refined and sensitive concentration. These things found expression in the instrumental forms and general style of chamber music. They led to the so-called "filigree" work of Brahms' music: the ingenious interweaving of parts obviously derived from the contrapuntal style, the compact phrase of closely moving voices, the crossing and interpenetrating of themes, harmonies and rhythms. Because of these peculiarities of style, Brahms used to be criticised as dry, scholastic, academic. He was in reality not so. A certain obscurity of construction and expression undoubtedly impaired the early success of his works. But as soon as that difficulty had been overcome, the listener conceived a strong liking for just this dreamy, inward sort of expression, which now came to be considered indicative of artistic sincerity.

Our task here is not to pass judgment, but to inquire into the individual characteristics of the different composers and see how these characteristics affect their creative activity. From this point of view Brahms was still the representative instrumental composer of the second half of the 19th century, the successor of Schubert, Mendelssohn and Schumann. Through his natural virility, he transformed the

youthful spirit of the early romanticists into the serious and sombre state of mind of the late romanticists.
In his loosening up of harmonic structure he was
like the great pre-classic masters, Bach in particular,
while at the same time, drawing his inspiration from
romanticism, he led the way to a new kind of harmonic activity. This recession of the purely harmonic
impulses of modulation and color and the reappear-
ance of independent voice-leading not only links the
romantic school with the pre-classical, but also
brings to light the first indication of the modern
trend in music.

It has been customary of late to contrast Brahms
with *Bruckner* and to call one or the other, according to taste, Beethoven's successor. But why should
we try to pick out a successor to Beethoven at all?
Beethoven is the colossal genius who dominates the
whole 19th century, the ideal of all its composers,
Wagner as well as Brahms, Liszt as well as Schumann,
Bruckner as well as Mendelssohn and Berlioz. But
none of them stands—if we may use the expression
—in intimate human contact with him. Opera composers in this respect trace back to Weber, German
instrumental composers to Schubert. Both Brahms
and Bruckner are descended from Schubert. If
Brahms gained his deeper inspiration from the pre-
classical masters, via Mendelssohn and Schumann,
Bruckner gained his from Wagner, whose dynamics
of modulation and color he remodelled into his sym-

phonic form. In giving vent to his imagination through his organ-like orchestra, with all its dramatic elements acquired from romantic music, he created a number of symphonies and religious works which incline towards a new type of cult music with a universal appeal.

Bruckner's particular significance lies in his having made use of the most subjective elements of romanticism in the expression of popular feeling and naïvely religious faith. For this reason also his music seems to many of us to possess a calm and tranquil quality. He differs from Brahms in the first place by the inevitable grandeur of his form, for as a composer of the expansive type he strove for symphonic structure, while the concentration of chamber-music forms was foreign to his nature. The intellectual and psychological factors in romanticism were equally alien to him. Here again he differs significantly from Brahms. Through the simplicity of his feeling Bruckner is the first to return to the expression of an impersonal, a universal attitude. This it is which gives him his religious trend and gives his music its tranquillity. The religious longing was common to all romanticists; the more their intensely subjective attitude towards life and art estranged them from it, the more ardently they sought it. It appears in the early romanticists of literature who frequently embraced Catholicism. It appears in the romanticists of music

as well, in Wagner, Bruckner, Brahms. It manifests
itself in a tendency toward mysticism, or, as with
Schumann, toward spiritism and the occult. It is
particularly evident in *Liszt,* who in his expression of
it is the very antithesis of Bruckner.

Like Bruckner, Liszt was a devout Catholic. But
his belief was not so utterly naïve as Bruckner's. It
was the searching, skeptical, gnawing faith of the intellectual romanticist with a somewhat worldly inclination. It determined the trend of his creative
activity from the "Faust" and "Dante" symphonies
to the "Gran Cathedral" mass, the oratorios of
"Christus" and "The Legend of Saint Elizabeth," and
many smaller compositions. Like Mendelssohn, Spohr
and Wagner, Liszt was one of the great practical
organizers of public musical activity. He thought of
the artist as a sort of prophet—and he saw himself
as one—who passes through the stages of virtuoso
and champion of everything new and good, to become the high-priest, the mediator between God and
man. This was the course Liszt's own life took. It was
dominated by the idea of service, as Wagner's was
by the idea of conflict, Bruckner's by that of worship and Brahms' by that of the evanescence of all
earthly things. When individuality has been exploited
to the limit of its possibilities, the desire for a common unity grows up once more. This great, unrealiz-
able spiritual longing is innate in all romanticists,

leads them always further in their individual ways, and thus determines the deeply pessimistic character of all romantic art.

With Wagner, Liszt, Brahms and Bruckner, what may be called the *high* or *late* romantic period comes to an end. It is followed by a period of disintegration which again produces a variety of characteristic reactions. These are most striking in the realm of opera as reactions against Wagner. The national differentiation which was one of the fundamental features of romanticism had been endangered by the triumphant progress of Wagner's operas all over the world. In the Latin countries this instrumentally conceived opera was looked upon as an alien type and for this reason the reaction against it came from Italy and France.

In Italy, through the influence of Bizet's "Carmen" upon the realistic style, a new sort of opera, known as the *veristic* type, came to life. With it realism abandoned itself absolutely to purely concrete representation. The effort at brevity and direct attack extended even to the outer form of the compositions in question, for which the one-act structure was chosen. So the two most famous works of this type—Mascagni's "Cavalleria Rusticana" and Leoncavallo's "Pagliacci"—appeared as a relief from the overburdensome ideas and musical psychology of Wagner's works. But the ablest composer Italy produced after Verdi was *Puccini,* whose talent was of a more

enduring quality than either Mascagni's or Leoncavallo's. He subjected the diminutive veristic forms to
a careful stylization and built them into the larger
opera of several acts, seeking always to preserve the
immediate charm of the moment in music and action
through ingratiating melody and continual dramatic
suspense.

Akin to Puccini, but artistically far more highly
cultured, was the Frenchman, *Debussy*. He was distinctly inspired by the posthumous works of Mussorgski, which were only gradually becoming known.
Mussorgski's "Boris Godunov" in particular preached
a new æsthetic gospel in the prominence it gave to
primitive folk melody and rhythm and to an unaf-
fected simplicity of expression. These influences,
combined with the Frenchman's natural instinct for
form derived from the rhythmic quality of his language and with certain carefully diluted Wagnerian
ideas, gave birth to "Pelléas and Mélisande," the typical French opera of the end of the century. It is a
thoroughly romantic work, conceived of harmonic
color, but color which dissolves in a delicate variety
of twilight tints. The psychological elements upon
which it rests are also dissipated in the dusk of mysticism. In "Pelléas and Mélisande" French opera re-
turned from the expansive pathos of Wagner to the
lyric contour which is specifically French, and which,
already cultivated in the works of Gounod and
Thomas, is now revived, through the influence of

Mussorgski's naturalism, in an impressionistic freedom of form.

Thus new and characteristically national forms came into being in France and Italy through the repudiation of German influence. Simultaneously *Russian* music began to affect West European culture more strongly than before. In Bohemia, *Smetana*, with his folk operas and instrumental works, created a national Czech music; in England and in the Scandinavian countries the newer Latin challenged the older German influence; national differentiation extended to the Balkan States and even to America. German music was still entirely dominated by the great late-romanticists, around whom partisan groups had formed, dividing the academic romanticists from the "new German school" following Wagner, Liszt and Berlioz. Brahms himself stood aloof from all partisanship, though he could not prevent the opponents of the new school from claiming him for their party, the more since no other suitable individual of sufficient importance was available. But since true creative genius will not long submit to partisan command in æsthetic matters, the younger artists in each faction gradually drifted into the opposing camp, party lines were obliterated, and some of the followers of both Wagner and Brahms even turned for inspiration towards the influences emanating from Italy and France. The common characteristic of all these composers is the continued expansion of harmonic activity from within which, now that pure modulation has been exploited to the utmost extent through increased use of chromatics, strives primarily towards development of color, of the shifting hues and shades of tone.

In order to preserve our historical point of view and keep out of the critical field, I shall name and briefly characterize the most important composers only. *Richard Strauss,* the ablest and most influential member of the new German school, succeeded Wagner and Liszt as a composer of opera and concert music. In Strauss the virtuosity which was a feature of early romanticism again stands out. The personal experience which had been the incentive and the strength of the late romantic masters, now finds expression in a greater technical skill. Hence Strauss turns gradually away from the romantic to the classic models, and to those of Mozart in particular, a process which indicates not a fundamental change of attitude, but the development of virtuosity to the point where it represents the perfection of artificial simplicity.

As Strauss stands in relation to Liszt and Wagner, so *Reger* stands in relation to Brahms. But Reger never attained the intrinsic clarity and masterly control of his medium that Strauss achieved; for his life's work, as various as it was uneven, ceased suddenly, unfulfilled. *Mahler,* the third of this group, was influenced by both Bruckner and the new German school. He was the symphonic representative of vanishing romanticism in contrast to Reger, who thought essentially in terms of chamber music. His compositions combine the influences of his predecessors, from Schubert to Liszt and Bruckner, but turn away from the religious piety of Bruckner to a new world-brotherhood of love.

While the dissolution of romanticism as well as the trend towards classical and pre-classical ideas may be seen in the music of Strauss, Reger and Mahler, *Pfitzner*, following upon Humperdinck who acts as a connecting link, achieves a sort of synthesis of the late romanticism of Wagner with the early romanticism of Schumann. This leads to a revival of romantic subjectivism, which finds expression in a rigid adherence to the immediate past. Finally in *d'Albert*, and more especially in *Schreker*, the amalgamation of German romanticism with French and Italian opera is clearly apparent. The symphonic structure remains, but it is gradually penetrated more and more by the trend towards melodious expression in song. The instrumentally conceived opera of the harmonic era once more approaches the original type of scenic song-play. The beauty of modulation dissolves completely in the colorful play of melody, all dramatic elements are calculated to arouse the sensuous appeal of music, the singing voice becomes the leading fac-

tor. Thus all the subjective, *specifically romantic*
characteristics of romantic opera are exaggerated to
the point of their own destruction, and from the ruins
rises once more the pre-classical ideal of *musical*
opera, opera to be sung.

CHAPTER XX

MODERN TRENDS

THE preceding chapter has brought us down to our own times. Perhaps the reader expected more detailed information about Hugo Wolf, Richard Strauss, Reger, Mahler, Pfitzner, Schreker, whereas these particular composers have been discussed collectively. I have intentionally avoided any sort of critical estimate, the purpose of these pages being to consider music history not in detail but as a whole. Even in treating of the music of the 18th century by describing the individual composers, no exception to this plan was made, for each of these composers is a complete entity in himself, representing the whole trend of his time. Brahms once most truly said of the masters of the 18th century: "They are the gods, we are the human beings." They had to become gods, since they lived not only their own lives but the life of all mankind. They represent a unique occurrence in man's intellectual history, revealing supreme potentialities, and making the 18th century a period of overwhelming greatness.

This is a fact we have to recognize. And yet there is no sort of transformation by which we can return

again to that great era. We may indeed copy the rules
its great men followed in their compositions, but we
cannot recreate the conditions which made possible
and justifiable the application of those rules. We can
also take a Stradivarius violin apart, ascertain its exact proportions and build a new instrument in ac-
cordance with them, but even with the highest skill
the best result we should attain would still be an imitation of Stradivarius. This way is not our way: *our*
way must lead forward. We must show no false con-
ceit of progress; but we must continue to *produce* to
the full extent of those abilities with which we have
been endowed, be they great or small. It is not for
us to quarrel with the place history has allotted us;
we must maintain that place and fill it. Then we shall
eventually come to learn how closely all times are
related to each other. We shall see that we not only
exist now but have been existing for a long time
and shall in turn always continue to exist; that all
phenomena are but the eternal interplay of creative
forces, which, themselves unchanging, ceaselessly dis-
unite but to combine anew.

The object of these chapters has been, as stated in
the beginning, not to give historical facts—since I am
neither an historian nor a teacher—but to show how
this process mainfests itself in the history of music
as the constant metamorphosis of musical forms. I
wished also to point out the folly of the idea of evolution which would make such changes appear as ab-

solute improvements. Looking back over the sequence of events here discussed, we see them pictured in a wave-like motion which repeats itself through the centuries. The crest of each wave represents a height, and by this very token carries in itself the tendency to fall; and each trough between two waves represents a low point which, in turn, carries in itself the tendency to rise. Thus periods which we describe as times of special glory contain within them the germs of their own decay, and those we describe as times of decay harbor the forces of revival. The separate steps of this process we are unable to detect. But experience teaches us that all forces, destructive as well as constructive, must always be present equally in the life of man, that growth and decay are in truth identical. The change from one to the other is but a change in appearance, a transformation, while the essential forces involved remain the same. Upon the recognition of this fact, as explained in the first chapter, I have sought to base the historical observations and conclusions here presented, and in this light I have tried to show how musical forms come into being and pass on.

Now we have reached our goal, if such observations may be said to have a goal at all. We have come to the consideration of the forms which belong to our own times, and which are therefore most easy to observe but perhaps the most difficult of all for us to understand. It is scarcely possible for us to take account of all the many composers in our midst. We cannot even be sure which of them possesses a surviving vitality. Probably we do not yet realize much that is important, while much that is unimportant looms large to our vision. Criticism, books, discussion, rather confuse than enlighten us. We hear a young composer praised on the one hand as extraordinarily gifted, while on the other he is declared to be a bungler and a charlatan. Catchwords are current: we speak of expressionistic, futuristic, atonal, polyharmonic or linear music. If we ask people what they mean by these words, most of them are embarrassed and unable to explain. There is a widespread opinion that the new music is on the wrong path. It is compared with the music of Bach, Haydn, Mozart and Beethoven, and since their music is recognized as beautiful it is logical to conclude that the new music, which sounds entirely different, is simply ugly. Not only the workings of the law of inertia upon the critic, but the relative nature of beauty, the variability of its components, are quite overlooked. We forget that Bach, Haydn, Mozart and Beethoven were just as modern in their times as our young composers are today. We forget that these young composers write music that is different not because they want to but because they *must*. And they must, because different perceptive powers live and thrive within them, and because in this very state of being different the creative energy of .life finds its expression.

This is not said in criticism or in commendation of any particular composer, but applies to the new music in general. Schumann, the enthusiastic champion of everything vital, once said: "If Mozart were alive today he would write piano concertos not of the type Mozart wrote but of the type Chopin wrote." This applied to a time in which Chopin was considered a revolutionary. Wherefore we may safely say that if Bach and Mozart, Beethoven, Schubert and Wagner were alive today, they most certainly would write not the kind of music we buy from the music-dealer as theirs, but an entirely different kind. It would probably be very much like the music we protest against today, calling their very names to witness. This I have felt obliged to say before attempting to define the nature of that which we now call the *new music,* a venture which the foregoing observations should justify us in making. If the new music is no mere arbitrary innovation, but a transformation once more, then it should be possible to discover the conditions which lie at the root of this change and the active impulses which have brought it about.

The last great epoch in music history begins about the middle of the 16th century and reaches up to the present time. These four centuries represent the period of *harmonic instrumental music.* Harmony and instrumental tone condition each other. Harmony is latent in instrumental tone, and its manifestation is an essentially instrumental phenomenon. I have tried to show how the development of harmony into artistic musical forms is determined by *three* different dynamic impulses; first, where the main emphasis is on the progression of the bass, the bass-tone itself being the foundation from which the harmony emanates; secondly, where the main emphasis is on melody, and harmony is the structure supporting the melodic line which constitutes the leading impulse of the music; and finally, where the main emphasis is on the middle voices and the harmony is forced apart, from the center downward towards the bass and upwards towards the melody, as it were, by means of modulation. This last procedure I have defined as the dispersion of harmony from within; it might even be more strongly described as a driving asunder, an atomising of the harmonic structure. It is strikingly expressed in the modulations of *Max Reger* and in the color effects of *Franz Schreker*.

Arrived at this point, we now ask: *what next?* There must certainly be further possibilities of harmonic development in modulation and color. But we may assume that romanticism has exhausted the essentials, and that any further extensions possible on the old foundation can be no more than exercises in variety of detail. Does this imply that we have reached the limit of harmonic possibilities, and that the three sources of dynamic activity—the bass, the melodic line, the modulating middle voices—are played out?

In a certain sense this is true. Let us say, therefore, that dynamic activity in this particular direction has been exhausted. So far the dynamic tendency has been towards expansion. From the time of Bach and Handel, indeed from the beginning of harmonic composition up to the present, the development of harmonic forms has always been essentially expansive, beginning with the vertical extension of the bass line, proceeding thence to the more pliable horizontal upper line of the melody, and ending in the outward overflow of the middle lines. Today we are witnessing the reversal of this process. The dynamic tendency is towards *contraction*. The great wave of harmonic expansion is rolling back, back to its starting point or perhaps even farther—this we cannot yet say with certainty. But we see the reverse motion, feel the compressing force unmistakably; therefore let us try to understand it. It is rooted in the very nature of harmonic music. If our previous definition of the nature of harmonic music has been correct, then it will also confirm the organic soundness of the present tendency.

In explaining how harmonic forms came into being, I said that harmony is not polyphonic, does not consist of independent voices as the old polyphonic vocal music does, but is *homophonic*, derived from the breaking up of the single tone into its overtones. The harmonic conception of tone may be likened to a prism by which light is split up into its component colors. Hence all harmonic forms are based upon a fundamental principle of division, of dispersion, or, as has been said above, of *dynamic expansion*. The reverse movement must, therefore, be based upon a fundamental principle of contraction, of *compression*. The object of this compression must be to regain the original unity of a tone out of its multiple subdivisions. Form is no longer derived through the prismatic breaking-up of tone in harmony. The aim of the creative impulse is to present tone in its original undivided entirety, in the form, for instance, in which it underlay the old polyphonic music.

Now a similar impulse exists in harmonic music too, in so far as its dynamic pattern is based upon the dispersion and re-gathering of tonal forces. From this re-gathering the cadence is derived. As suggested in our discussion of Wagner, the further afield the modulation is carried, the more important is the cadence through which the harmonic threads are once more collected. It was this re-assembling of tonal forces in the cadence which caused all romantic music to express the idea of solution, of redemption. Yet as the cadence aimed at achieving an effect of contrast, it implied that harmonic activity covering a wide range must necessarily have taken place first. Here we see the link between the new music and the music of romanticism, and also the contrast between them. This great substructure of harmonic activity, for the creation of which the romantic composer needed his personal reaction to experience and in which he proved the individuality of his art, now ceases to exist. Only the cadence itself is left, as it were, the process by which the scattered tonal forces of harmony are brought together and carried on as newly established units. The new music begins, in a way, to take form, where romantic music stops—namely at the gathering process of the cadence—whence it proceeds to its own further development. In so doing, however, it has recourse once more to polyphonic devices.

I have tried to define the principle underlying the new musical forms without taking into consideration any particular composers or compositions. In actual composition this principle is not so distinct as here presented. The composer has not adopted it deliberately, yet it is manifest in a variety of ways, mingled always with his own individual characteristics as well as with elements surviving from the past. But since we are discussing the new music in general, and the change it illustrates, we have the right to seek a formula by which to describe its essential nature by generalizing from certain observations we have repeatedly made. Thus we are first aware of a movement in the opposite direction from that in which the process of harmonic expansion has been carried on. I should call

this movement not a retrogression, not a retracing of
steps, but a continuation over the opposite half of
the globe, as it were, towards the antipodes. It tends
away from harmonic dispersion towards unification;
it perceives a tone, in other words, not as part of a
harmonic complex but as an independent unit in
itself.

From this tendency *Busoni* derived his idea of a re-
newed classicism, meaning the supremacy of *melody*
once more and the technique of thematic development, as against harmonic expansion. According to
our earlier observations, this idea would represent a
return to the second stage of harmonic form, in
which the melodic upper voice was the leading factor.
From the same impulse, furthermore, springs the evident relationship to Handel and especially to Bach,
which we observe in *Schönberg* and the younger composers as well as in Busoni. According to our earlier
observations, again, this process would represent a
return to the first stage of harmonic form, in which
the fundamental bass voice was the leading factor.
But though these movements seem to return to the
older forms, they do not imitate them, or they would
perforce tend toward harmonic expansion. They take
over these older forms, rather, to use them in their
own way. It is both idle and dangerous to prophesy;
yet the tendency of this movement is so unmistakable that I feel justified in expressing the opinion that
it will not stop at Bach and Handel. It may even lead

beyond their music, which is still harmonic, further back into the past to the point of time where tone was not yet harmonically divided—back, that is, to the old, the *true polyphony*. Only then would the great circle be closed, which began with the unified tone of ancient music, led through polyphony to the overtones of harmony, through Bach and Handel, through the Viennese classicists, to the further dispersion of this harmonic tone by the romanticists, and thence back again by way of the new music to unified tone once more.

The question of the *medium* through which this newly unified tone may be expressed should also be considered. If harmonic and instrumental music are synonymous, if instrumental tone is a manifestation of this prismatic breaking up of tone, then the undivided tone, which again encloses all tonal energies within itself, would have to be not instrumental but *vocal*. Instrumental tone could in this case function only in some subservient capacity, as it did in the great days of vocal music, though in a totally different way, of course, as yet unguessed.

We must not abandon ourselves too freely to dreams of what the future may bring forth, sure though we may be of the wave-like motion of events and the return it always involves. Yet we may note that there is a distinct inclination today to recognise the characteristic quality of vocal tone and its susceptibility to construction in forms fundamentally different from those of instrumental tone. An especially significant indication of this tendency is to be seen in the reawakening of interest in the old opera which was built purely upon the distinctive quality of vocal tone, and in Handel's operas particularly. Another indication is to be seen in the newly awakened interest in the treatment of the voice apparent in the present day opera of Strauss, Schreker and the younger composers. Even the idea so much in favor today of the contrast between Wagner and Verdi, which we have seen cannot be substantiated, has its root in the assertion of the rights of the voice as distinct from instrumental tone. The trend towards a reawakening of the vocal conception of tone is not a matter of speculation, but is already beginning to express itself in unmistakable signs.

There are still other evidences of this tendency to think of tone as contracted into a unit. We notice that harmonic expansion loses its force as the constructive principle, that it is no longer the dynamics of modulation and color which furnish the impetus to form, but, on the contrary, the urge towards contraction. Large musical forms and greatly augmented instrumental bodies now no longer have any justification for existence. Thus we see the great orchestra of the post-romantic era grow smaller and smaller until it becomes a chamber orchestra. We notice how the gigantic forms which Bruckner, Mahler, Strauss need for their music, which is still dominated by the idea of harmonic expansion, now contract, as it were. They shrink into small, clear-cut concentrated patterns, which are examples not of the aphoristic brevity of the early German romanticists, but of energy compressed to a high degree of intensity, just as the multiple harmonic constituents of the tone itself are now forced back into a single unit. If Busoni represents the melodic and Schönberg the contrapuntal type of form, I should call *Stravinsky* the most important exponent of this contracted or compressed type.

I believe that everything has herewith been said which can be said within the limits of the present study, in order to make clear the law of change which is at work within the new music. In closing, I would like to apply this law of change to some of the leading ideas that have been presented here. We have seen that in the course of music history characteristic national forms have always alternated with forms that represent a spiritual unity. The 19th century was a period of *national* music and therefore, in accord with our picture of the wave-like progress of events, the new music will strive toward *universality*. The 19th century was a period of *secular* music and therefore, according to the same law, the new music will be of the *cult* type—music with a universal spiritual appeal. The 19th century cultivated music in which the *emotional significance* of tone was paramount; the new music will instead reveal once more

the *essential quality* of the tone itself. The music of
the 19th century represented the last stage in the
harmonic expansion of tone that was *instrumentally
conceived;* the new music will represent the unified
intensity of tone that is *vocally conceived*. Even this,
if perfected, will not mean that music has reached its
goal. It will indicate not an ascent or a descent, a
climax or a decline, but a transformation, the change
which itself always gives birth to further change.
This is the great lesson taught us by the history of
art.

So we look back today to see the world of instrumental harmony vanishing into the past. As it disappears we think not of an antiquated style which we
have triumphed over and discarded, but of something beautiful that is no longer ours. In leaving it
behind we go in search of a new beauty, for, in the
words of Hyperion's Song of Fate,

> "It is given us
> Nowhere to rest."

INDEX

INDEX

Adam, 223.
d'Albert, 252.
Ambrosius, 48.
aria, 101, 157, 178.
Arnim, Bettina von, 188.
Auber, 223, 231.

Bach, Johann Sebastian, 23, 94, 106, 112 seq., 119 seq., 130, 132-
 136, 141, 144, 147, 153, 168, 194, 195, 201, 204, 213,
 240, 242, 245, 257, 258, 260, 263, 264.
Bach, Philipp Emanuel, 130, 142, 144, 149.
balatta, 62.
Beethoven, 19, 20, 31, 106, 113, 125, 134, 144, 168, 169, 182
 seq., 196, 199, 200, 204, 205, 209, 210, 211, 213, 217, 220,
 226, 245, 257, 258.
Bellini, 221, 222, 231, 233.
Berlioz, 205, 217 seq., 224, 226, 231, 241, 243, 245, 250.
Bizet, 209, 225, 227, 237 seq., 248.
Boieldieu, 223.
Bonaparte, Jerome, 187.
Brahms, 31, 125, 242-248, 250, 251, 254.
Bruckner, 31, 125, 242, 245, 247, 248, 252, 265.
Busoni, 263, 266.

caccia, 62.
cadence, 229 seq., 240 seq., 261 seq.
Calvin, 75.
Cherubini, 223.

Handel, 23, 94, 103, 106, 112 seq., 119 seq., 130, 133, 135, 136, 141, 153, 155-157, 166-168, 195, 201, 204, 240, 242, 243, 260, 263, 265.
harmony, 77, 78, 81, 90-92, 107 seq., 129, 203, 204, 228, 258 seq., 262.
harmony, instrumental, 98, 110, 149, 180, 234, 267.
Hasse, Johann Adolf, 158.
Haydn, 20, 106, 125, 130, 144 seq., 155, 168, 169, 180, 181, 184, 189, 190, 193-195, 199, 257.
Heine, 213.
Hérold, 223.
hexachords, 57, 58.
Homer, 188.
homophony, 62, 78, 81-83.
Humanists, 75.
Hummel, 217.
Humperdinck, 252.

Isaak, 81.

Kant, 189, 193.
Keiser, Reinhard, 103, 123.
Klopstock, 130.

Lassus, Orlandus, 69, 77, 81, 94.
Leoncavallo, 248, 249.
Lessing, 130.
Lied, 209 seq., 219.
Liszt, 215 seq., 226, 231, 241, 243, 245, 247, 248, 250-252.
Lully, 95, 165.
Luther, 75, 81, 82.

madrigal, 62.
Mahler, 48, 125, 251, 252, 254, 265.